praise for *whispers of humanity*

whispers of humanity delves deep into the psyche of personal potential with a clear resounding voice. Words married to colours, in a beautiful weave of evocative emotions and passionate paintings, lead us into a philosophical garden of vivid imagery and vibrant thoughts. The innate talents of Kyle Hawke and Wade Edwards, blended in verse and art, are monumental indeed and they shine like a wishing star on every polished page. When I finished perusing this book, digesting the words and drinking in the images, I felt an inner blessing stir in my soul, alive with the hue of hope and the posit of possibility.

Candice James
Poet Laureate Emerita
New Westminster, BC

Kyle Hawke and Wade Edwards have created a stunning combination of words and images that make every page of this beautiful book a surprise. The poems, like the paintings, are often abstract and impressionistic, making each entry the kind of surprise one usually finds when turning the corner in a garden filled with riotous, varied blooms. Poetic images and questions are juxtaposed over equally poetic and evocative colours and images that reflect the world we live in and the emotions we feel. Bravo.

Brad Fraser
Playwright/Director

At once raw and visceral, transcendent and luminous, *whispers of humanity* moves beyond the union of image and word to become a primer on being fully human. Seductively evoking all six senses, it casts its spell and we are drawn deep into its beating heart and we begin the journey to our own.

From fractured kaleidoscopes of colour to fragile sweeps of moth wings, ice crystals, the masterful placement of text within images is an artform in itself. We experience the alchemy of poetry, visuals, and juxtaposition.

This exceptional collection does not simper for the pretty and the pleasant, but intoxicates and entreats us, caresses and provokes us. Wielding metaphor and analogy with exquisite precision, it transforms the secular into the sacred, the mundane into the magical. It is entirely human.

Sylvia Taylor
Author of The Fisher Queen
and Beckoned by the Sea

praise for *whispers of humanity*

Poet Kyle Hawke has collaborated with the artist Wade Edwards to create work of great beauty and fire in their collaborative volume, *whispers of humanity*.

Kyle was able to balance the juxtaposition of multifarious colour and mood with his strong gift to choose the perfect word to connect with the reader's heart.

Both Kyle and Wade work with imagination to marry thought with form. From these artistic explorations, Kyle worked with many brushes to create both short and longer poems using his delicate subtlety and strong voiced authenticity.

This is a collection that traverses many landscapes, but always with a keen awareness of narrative and imagery.

This fine collection was made even more intense and lovely with the perfect union of art and word.

Jude Neale
Author of 7 books including
A Blooming

This merging of words and art is vibrantly alive. The combination of Wade Edwards' brightly colourful art with Kyle Hawke's spoken word poetry makes the words jump off the page in a way that's almost audible.

Heidi Greco
Author of Practical Anxiety

Johann Wolfgang von Goethe wrote, "A man should… read a little poetry, and see a fine picture every day of his life, in order that worldly cares may not obliterate the sense of the beautiful."

Poet Kyle Hawke and artist Wade Edwards' book, *whispers of humanity*, does just this. It provides an escape into the realms of the creative, finding meaning in Kyle's words while getting lost in Wade's imagery. I have always been a fan of artistic collaboration and the authentic expression it produces when paired befittingly.

The words seem to flow around the pages but are delightfully contained by the originative imagery that pulls, twists, fades, and at times controls the direction in which they appear to you.

Like a good evening cup of tea after a long day, I steeped myself in this book and thoroughly enjoyed the engaging and refreshing poetry and art that I was set adrift in.

James Picard
Artist/Director/Filmmaker

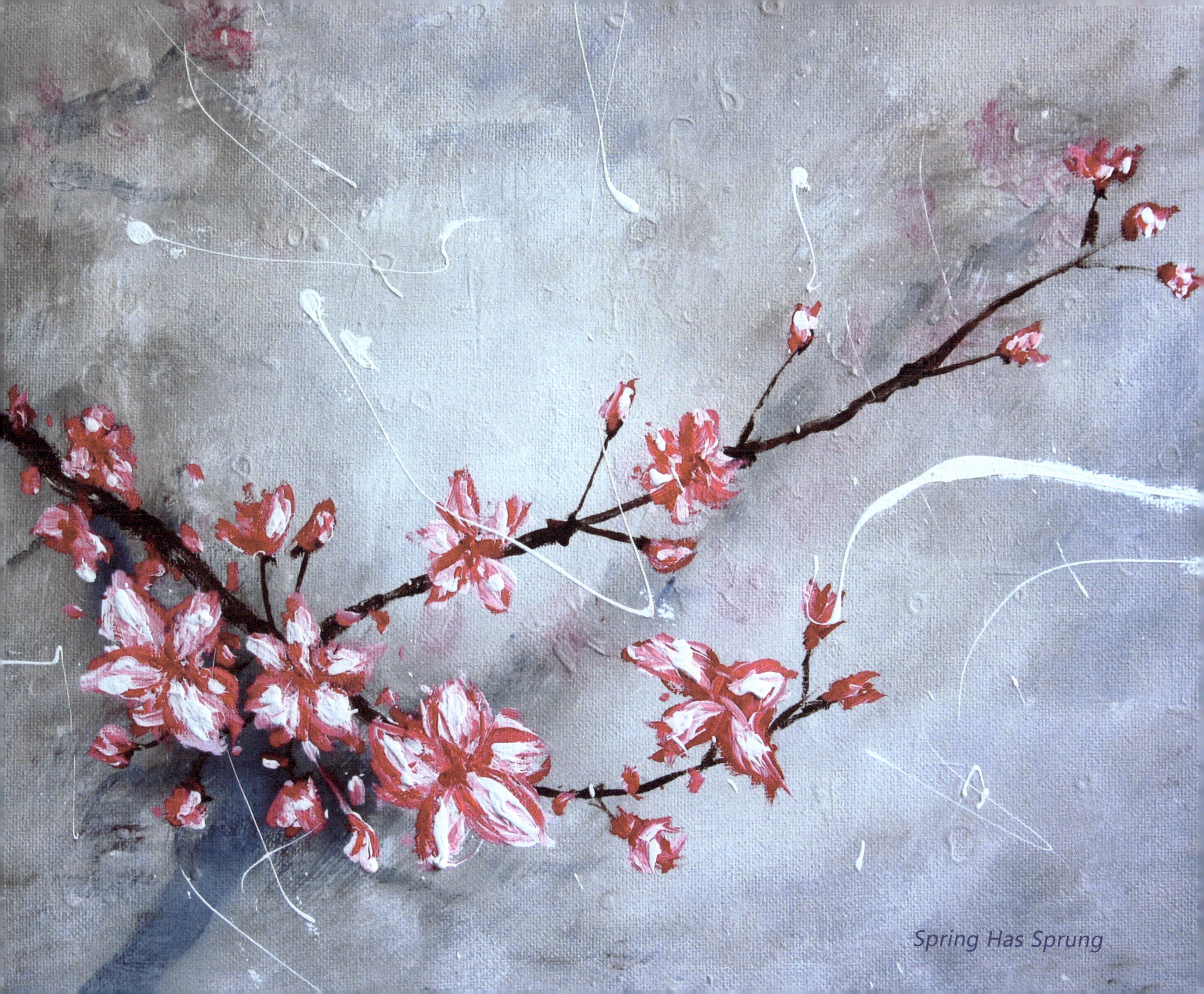
Spring Has Sprung

*whispers of
humanity*

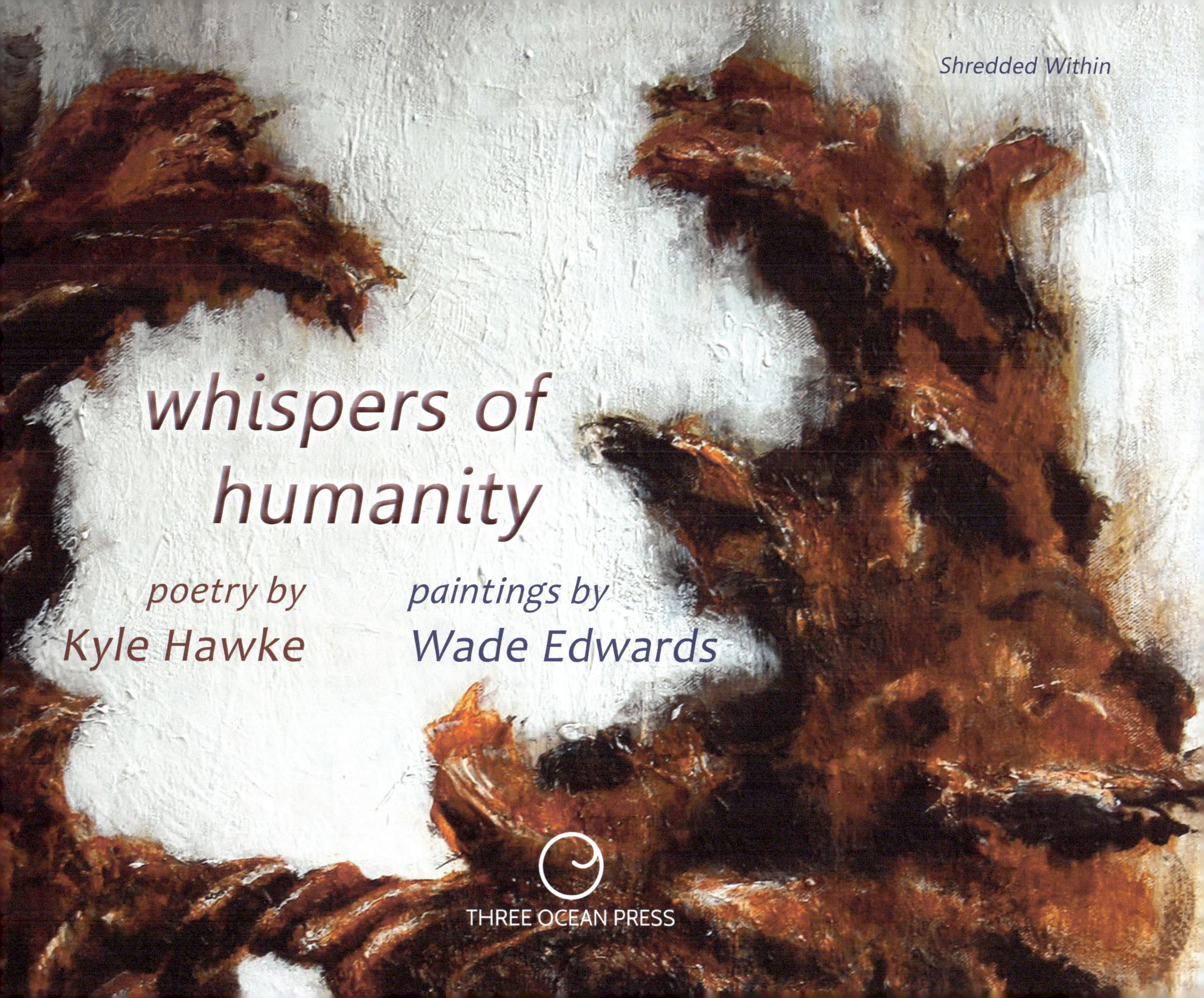
Shredded Within

whispers of
humanity

poetry by
Kyle Hawke

paintings by
Wade Edwards

THREE OCEAN PRESS

Library and Archives Canada Cataloguing in Publication

Title: Whispers of humanity / poetry by Kyle Hawke ; paintings by Wade Edwards.
Names: Hawke, Kyle, 1968- author. | Edwards, Wade, 1973- artist.
Identifiers: Canadiana (print) 20190122935 | Canadiana (ebook) 20190122943 | ISBN 9781988915159 (softcover) | ISBN 9781988915166 (HTML)
Classification: LCC PS8615.A8173 W55 2019 | DDC C811/.6—dc23

Editor: Bonnie Nish
Artistic Editor: PJ Perdue
Proofreader: PJ Perdue
Cover and Book Designer: Kyle Hawke
Front cover art: *Horizons* by Wade Edwards
Back cover art: *Fireflies* by Wade Edwards

Three Ocean Press
8168 Riel Place
Vancouver, BC, V5S 4B3
778.321.0636
info@threeoceanpress.com
www.threeoceanpress.com

First publication, August 2019

Dedications

For the Gathering Place Poets,
especially those who've gone:
Jerry Appleton,
John-Ward Leighton,
Muriel Marjorie,
Bud Osborn,
and Pete Schweitzer

Kyle Hawke

To Christy
and my children,
Kassidy,
Bryson,
Ocean-Lee,
and Damon
who inspire while
I create my art

Wade Edwards

If we were to thank all the poets, there would simply be too many to name. So let us thank the poetry itself, those words that make us think or feel in ways we hadn't thought or dared to previously.

If we were to thank all the painters, there would again simply be too many to name. So let us thank the paintings themselves, those images that show us how things really look below the surface, stripped of their trappings.

Kyle & Wade

Burgundy II

Contents

poems by Kyle Hawke · paintings by Wade Edwards

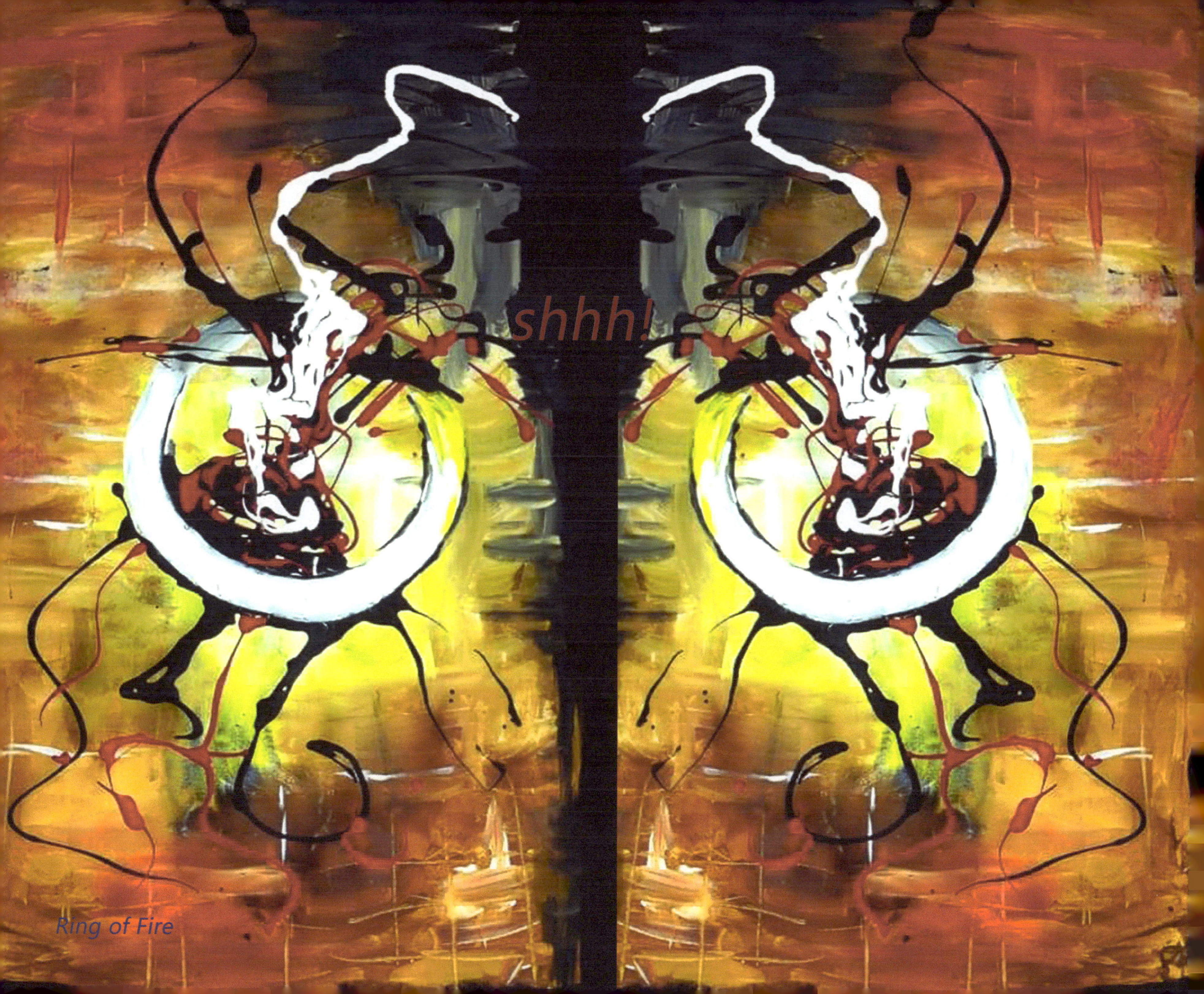

shhh!
Ring of Fire

shhh!
can you hear it?
that singular soulful solo that never ceases
that hum that hides in the heart of everything
        that song of silence?

shhh!
can't you feel it?
quell the qualms that cause question
while will waits in the womb of the undone
        sense the senselessness
        cease your struggle

                                    shhh!
                                    give in.
                                    shhh!
                                    give in.
                                    shhh!

                        be one with being
                        be one being with something to share
                            in the quiet calms
                            in the fragile falls of time
                            stumbling slowly towards too late

2   *Stormy Blue*

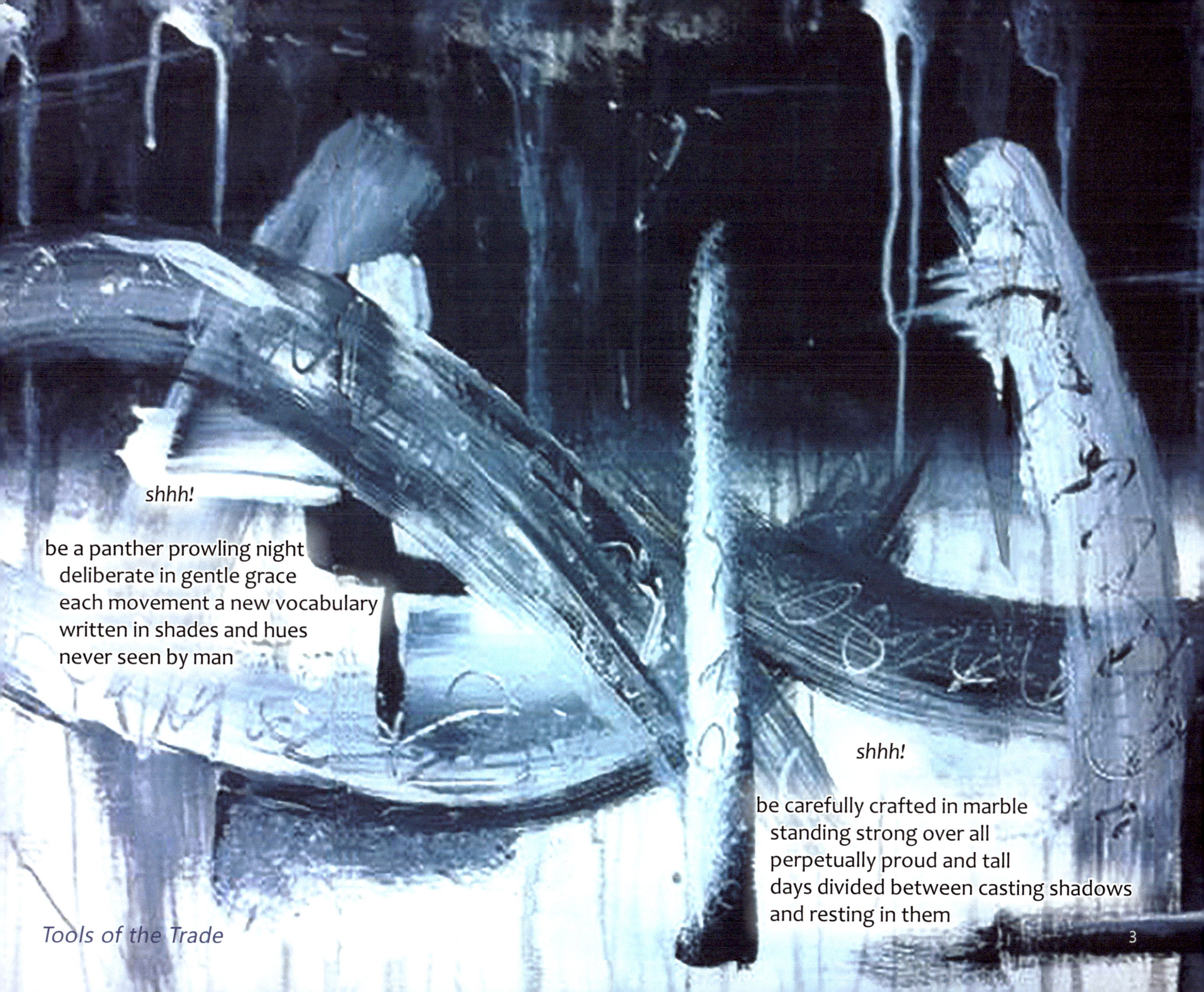

shhh!

be a panther prowling night
deliberate in gentle grace
each movement a new vocabulary
written in shades and hues
never seen by man

shhh!

be carefully crafted in marble
standing strong over all
perpetually proud and tall
days divided between casting shadows
and resting in them

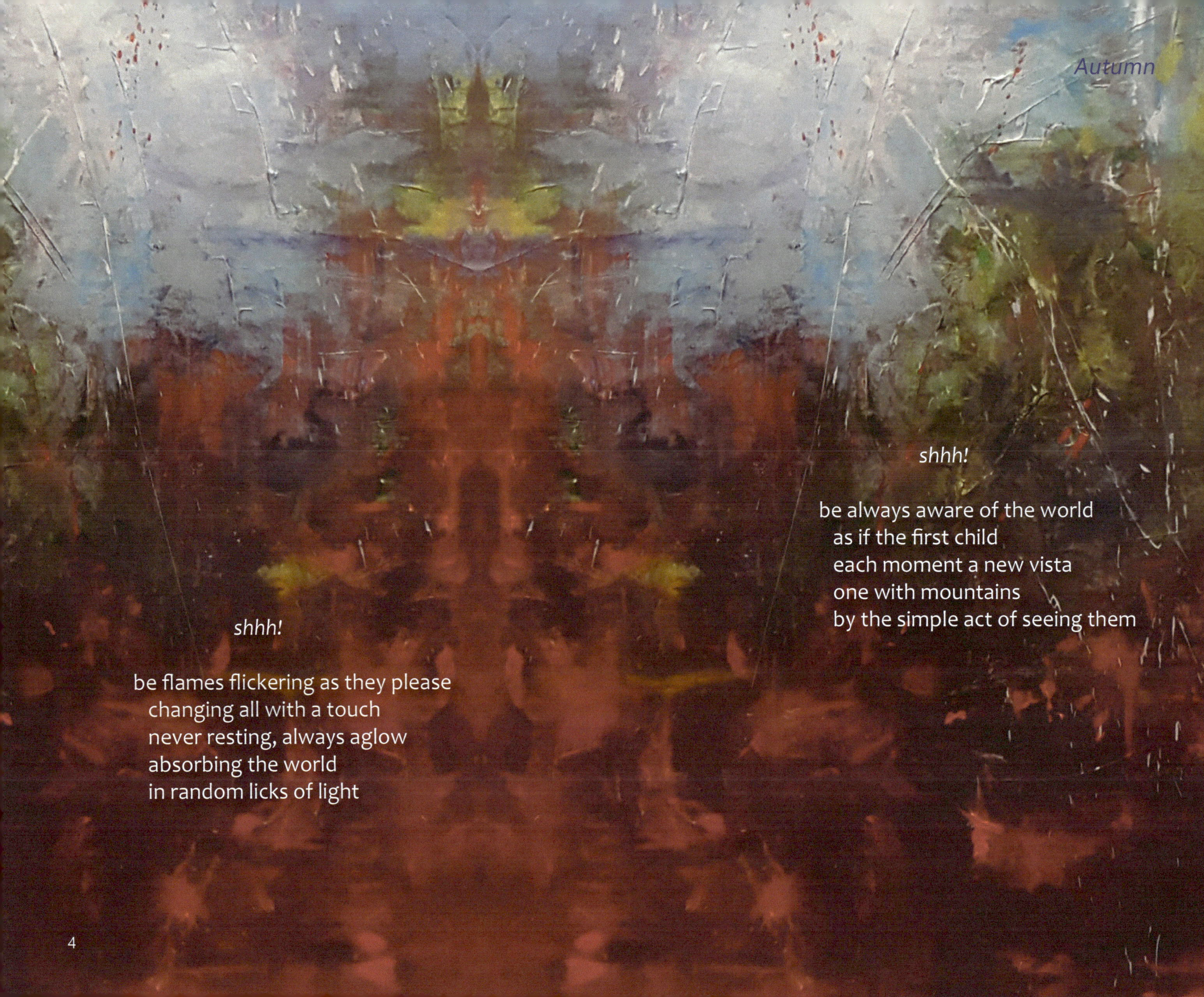
Autumn

shhh!

be always aware of the world
  as if the first child
  each moment a new vista
  one with mountains
  by the simple act of seeing them

shhh!

be flames flickering as they please
  changing all with a touch
  never resting, always aglow
  absorbing the world
  in random licks of light

4

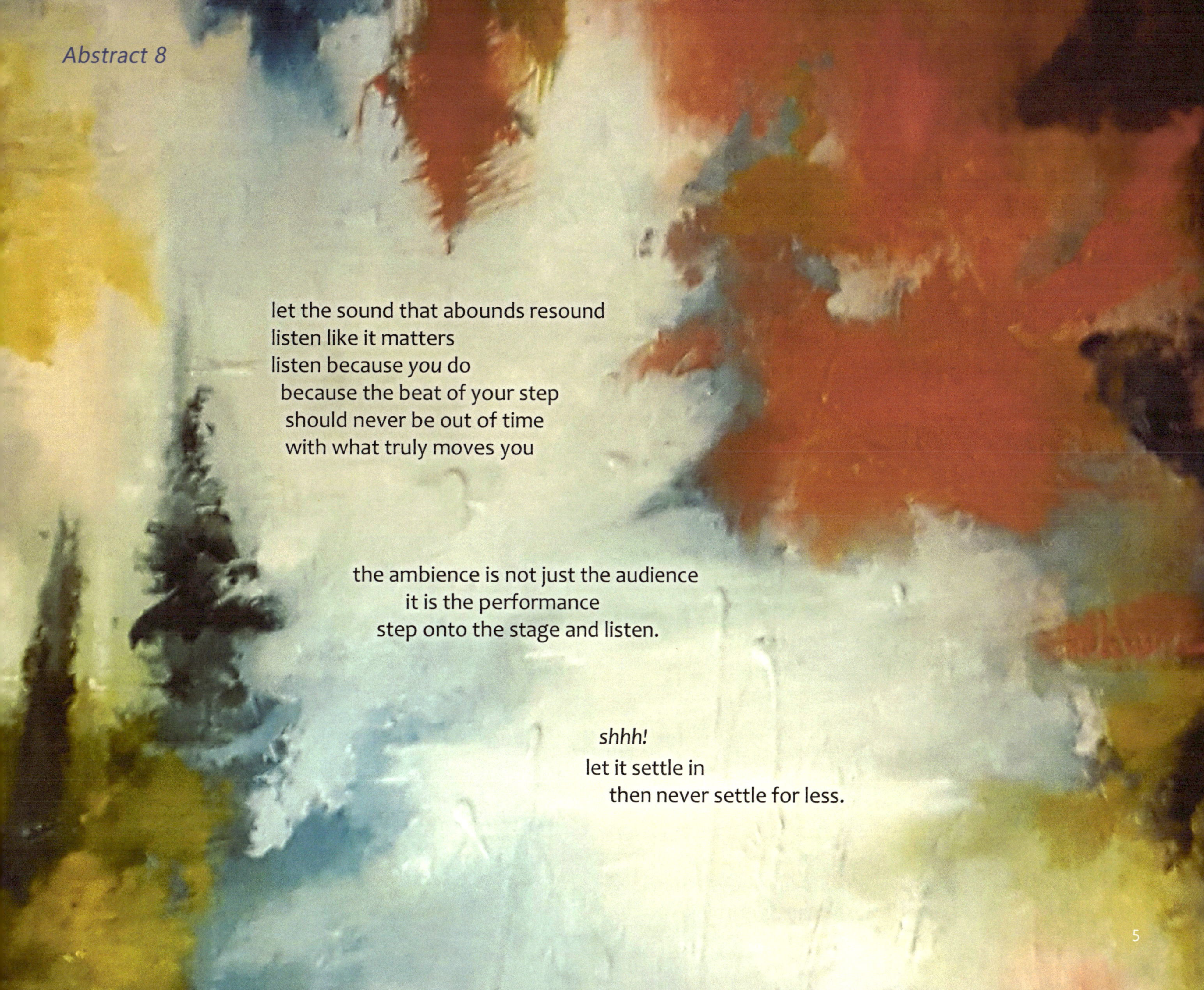

let the sound that abounds resound
listen like it matters
listen because *you* do
  because the beat of your step
  should never be out of time
  with what truly moves you

the ambience is not just the audience
it is the performance
step onto the stage and listen.

shhh!
let it settle in
then never settle for less.

building blocks

bricks and mortar
    shelter peasants and kings alike
  the basic building blocks
      make no separation by status
the same walls can enclose both dirt and gold

flesh and blood
    shelter peasants and kings alike
  the basic building blocks
      make no separation by status
the same heart can enclose both dirt and gold

      inside,
        we choose who we are
        what we will be
      and whatever that might mean

      outside, however,
        histories are built of sturdier stuff
        selecting very few to shelter
        very few to hold up
          above the muck and mire
          the rest of us trudge through

      and in that moment
        when one of the eyes of history
          catches you in its sight
        it is not 'as above, so below'
          it is all or nothing

when — if — your chance to rise arrives
  do not be shy
  do not let yourself
    feel small
sing your most secret songs
slay the giants who bedevil you
fire the muck and mire
      into bricks and mortar
and build an edifice
      that will house the future

    else, end up forgotten by time
      more base clay collecting on and weighting down
        the feet of those who will follow

      let them rise
     linger in the air like lilting chords
    belt out those notes which can shatter swords
      harmonize with the hum all about you
        mouth the hymn that heals the hurt
        duet with divinities
        do it
        do it now

      leave no notes for later
    no stains on paper
      that do not echo through the halls

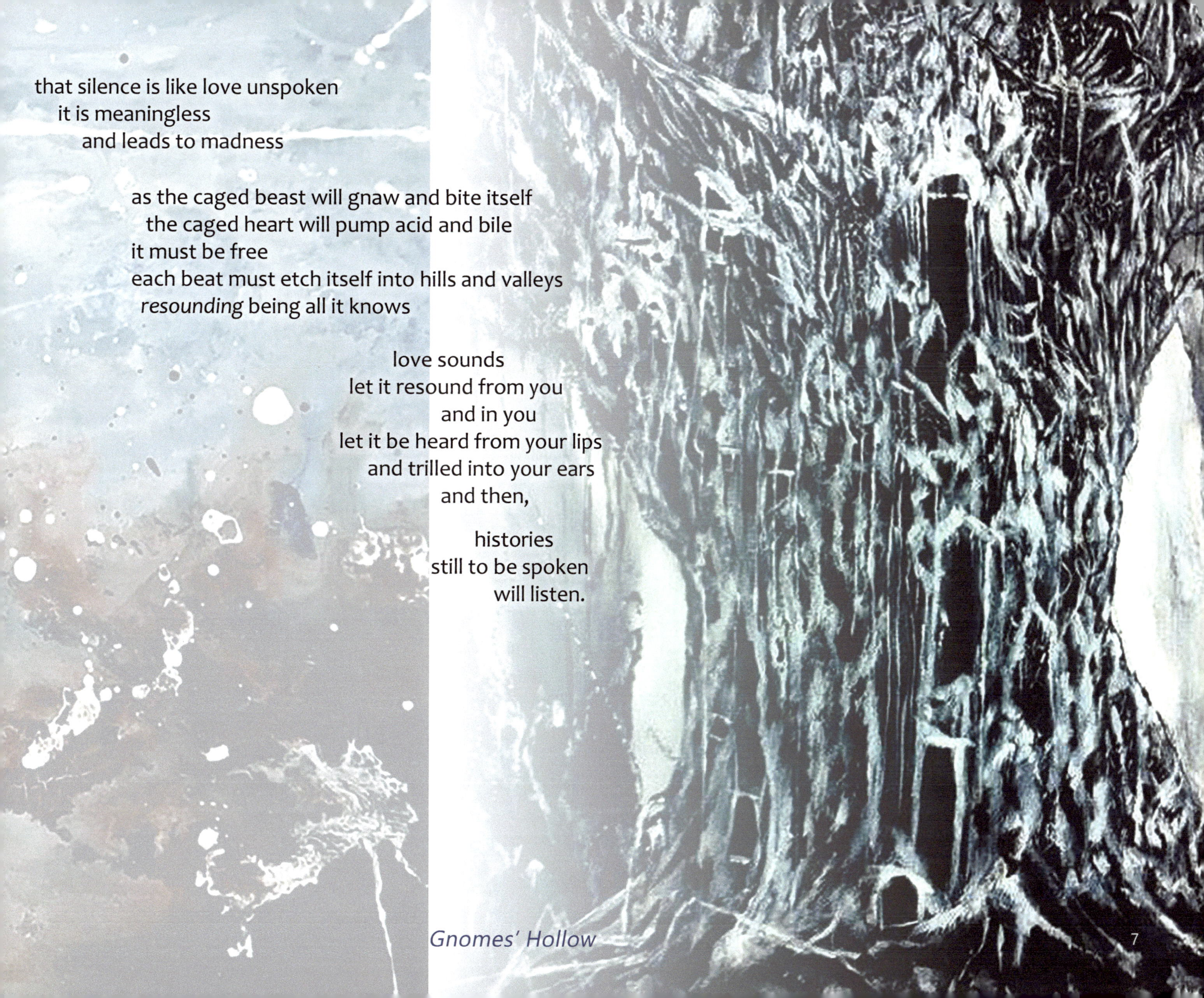

that silence is like love unspoken
  it is meaningless
    and leads to madness

    as the caged beast will gnaw and bite itself
     the caged heart will pump acid and bile
    it must be free
    each beat must etch itself into hills and valleys
    resounding being all it knows

        love sounds
        let it resound from you
          and in you
        let it be heard from your lips
         and trilled into your ears
         and then,

        histories
        still to be spoken
          will listen.

Gnomes' Hollow

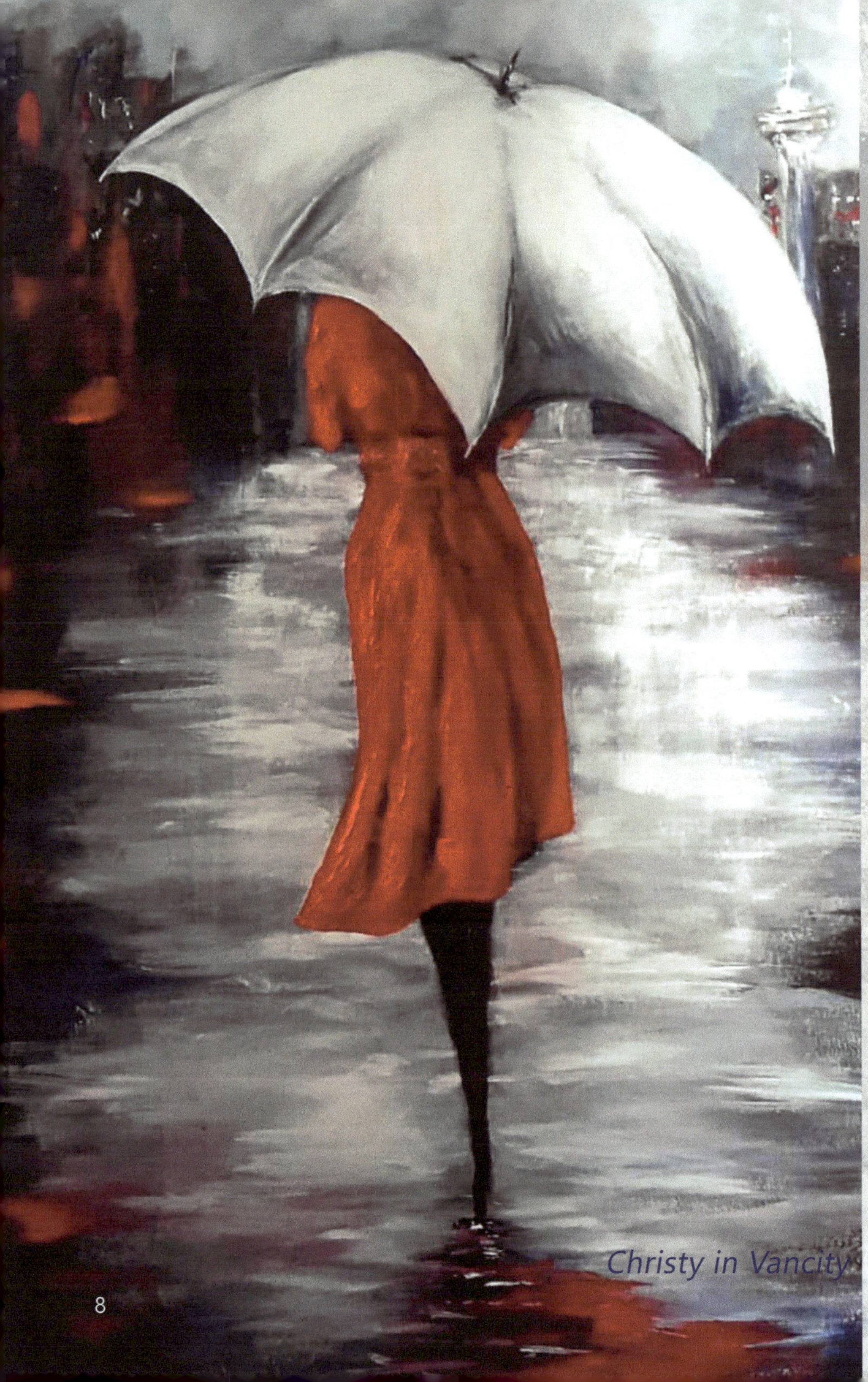

circles (in the square)

a circle in a circle in an oval
   so simple, so complex
the slightest movement says so much
       tells too many things

walking through the square
circles in circles in ovals in pairs
shift and scan, most seeing past you
but a few, telltale, bounce back on making contact

the traces of their passing remain
forming questions: *you? them?*
   are those clothes wrong?
    that hair unkempt?
    that mouth askew?
    the skin too strange?

are the subtleties seen misinterpreted?
that you live untrue or love unjust
or that they simply wonder if you do?
do their inquests introduce indecencies virally
    writing themselves into your cells
    challenging your defences?

are the subtleties you see misinterpreted?
are shallow searches once written onto you
now written onto others as response?

centered in the square
a pair of circles in circles in ovals
        catches yours
         responds with a smile
you know that you don't know why
you know that why doesn't matter
and a pair of ovals separated by a line
        curve

and you know the next
      pair of circles in circles in ovals
that trip when their journey intersects yours
        will be greeted similarly
and why won't matter
because why *couldn't* matter
so if something so simple, so complex
      will tell so many things
then those may as well be clear.

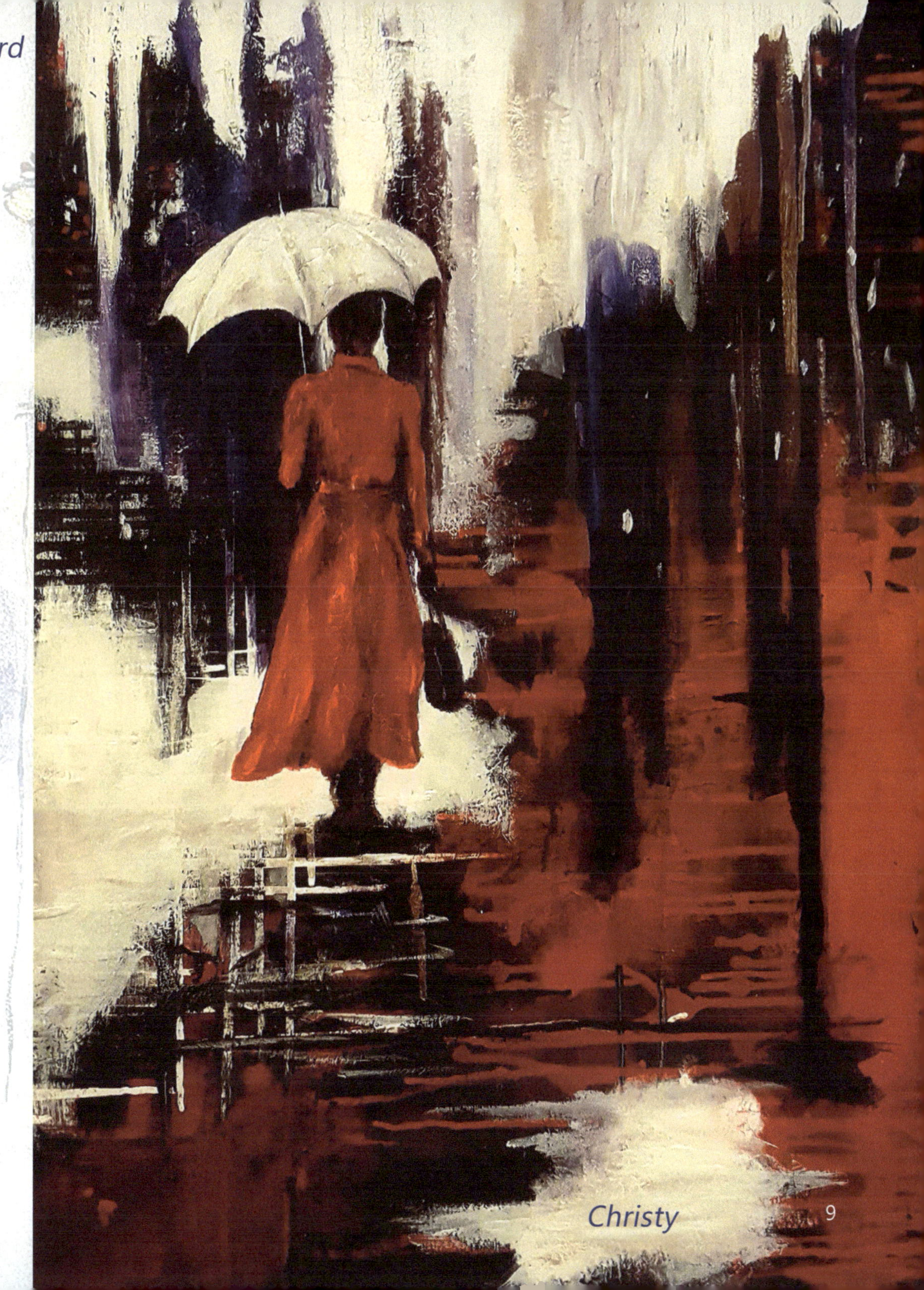

Christy

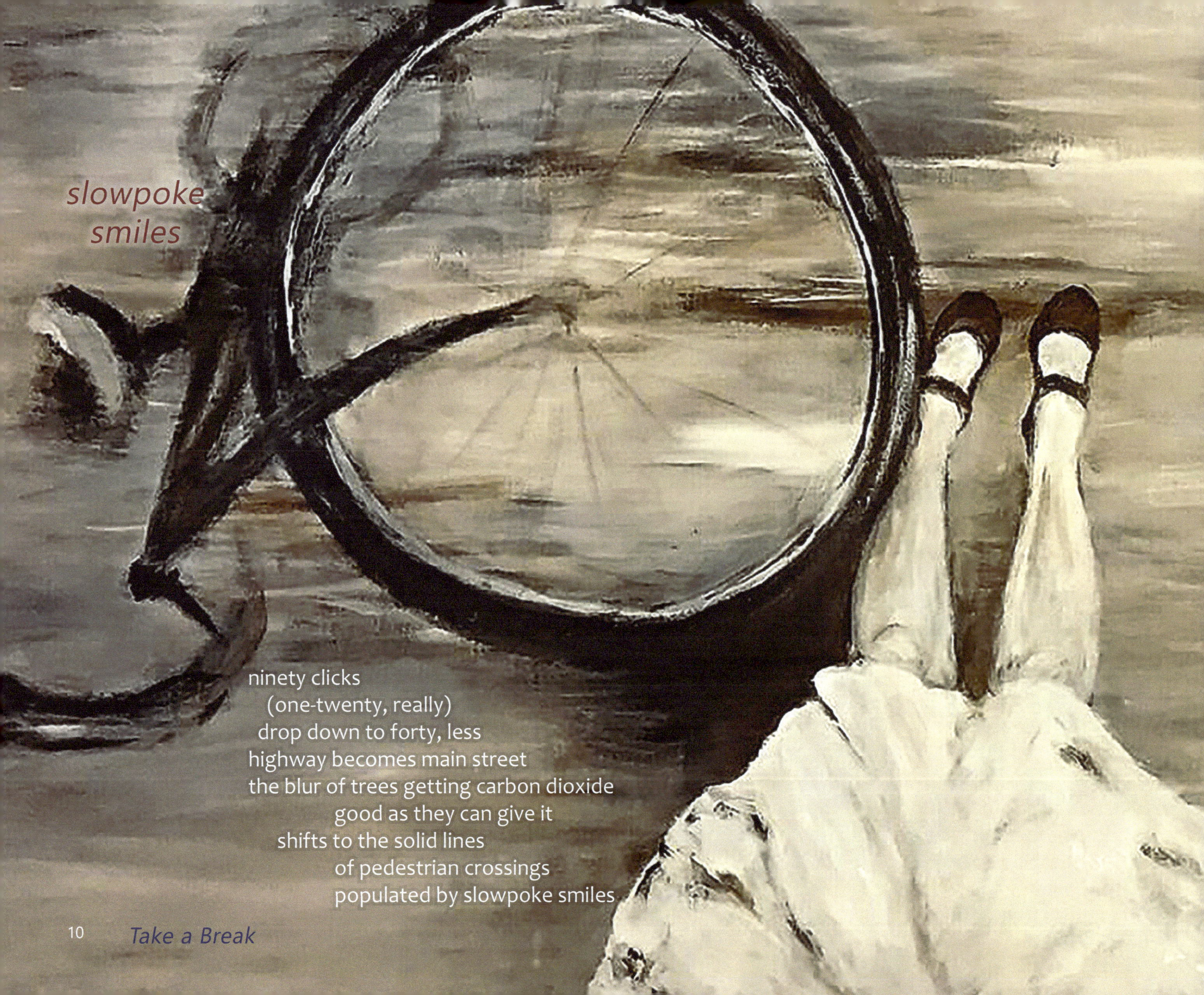
slowpoke
smiles

ninety clicks
   (one-twenty, really)
 drop down to forty, less
highway becomes main street
the blur of trees getting carbon dioxide
      good as they can give it
   shifts to the solid lines
      of pedestrian crossings
      populated by slowpoke smiles

they don't jaywalk
    no jaded urban jaundices here
the signs exclaiming '30'
    and the 'x's punctuating them
        — they know —
will have their strict grammar
interrupted by the dropped 'g's of an acura
    expecting them to pay the price of a freeway

that's just part of life in those towns
the ones that might have been
                built for something else
        but ended up just a point between a and b

they just warn their children
rather than put in speedbumps
because nothing can stand in the way
        of the automobile

after all, cars carry those weary travellers
            who subsidize the strip
stopping for the all-day breakfast at marie's diner
or picking up condoms at schulman's drugstore
    the locals pick those up out of town
        where they aren't recognized
        even if they make sure harry and joan
            get the rest of their business

and though some shop names have changed
— picking up recognizable national brands
all the better to cue in the passers-by —
they're still susan's or joe's or the flemings'
        if you're in the know

past that straight line meant for those
        who never meant to stop
the trees are noticeably prouder
    than their cousins only seen as blurs
they spend their days and nights
            pointing greenly up to clear skies
        with the unhurried wisdom of glaciers

past that straight line,
the rest of the streets wind and curl lazily
smiling mandalas and accidental geometry
    that only make sense if you know
        who used to live on the corner
        why settlers avoided that hill
        about those crazy plans that just
                    never
                    quite
                    happened

in those towns,
    people are used to things not quite happening
            the indefinite is the expectation
solidities are left to the urbanite
    except on main street
where two worlds coalesce, if not collide
        on that slow stretch too often taken too fast
and those slowpoke smiles on the crosswalk
hint at what that acura driver might never know
because you can't be grounded going one-twenty

peace is the province of the parked mind
    because no matter how fast you go
        it doesn't mean you'll get there.

Journeys End

tomorrow:
we wait
  and reach,
    stretching whatever's necessary to get there
      a promise *and* a threat

like tomorrow itself —
twenty-four hours journey
to an unknown destination
for unknown reasons,
unknowing reasonings
beckoning with
and warning of
the loss of today

it seems impossible as we try but never close our hands
about that prize
as we are loath to admit time exceeds our grasp

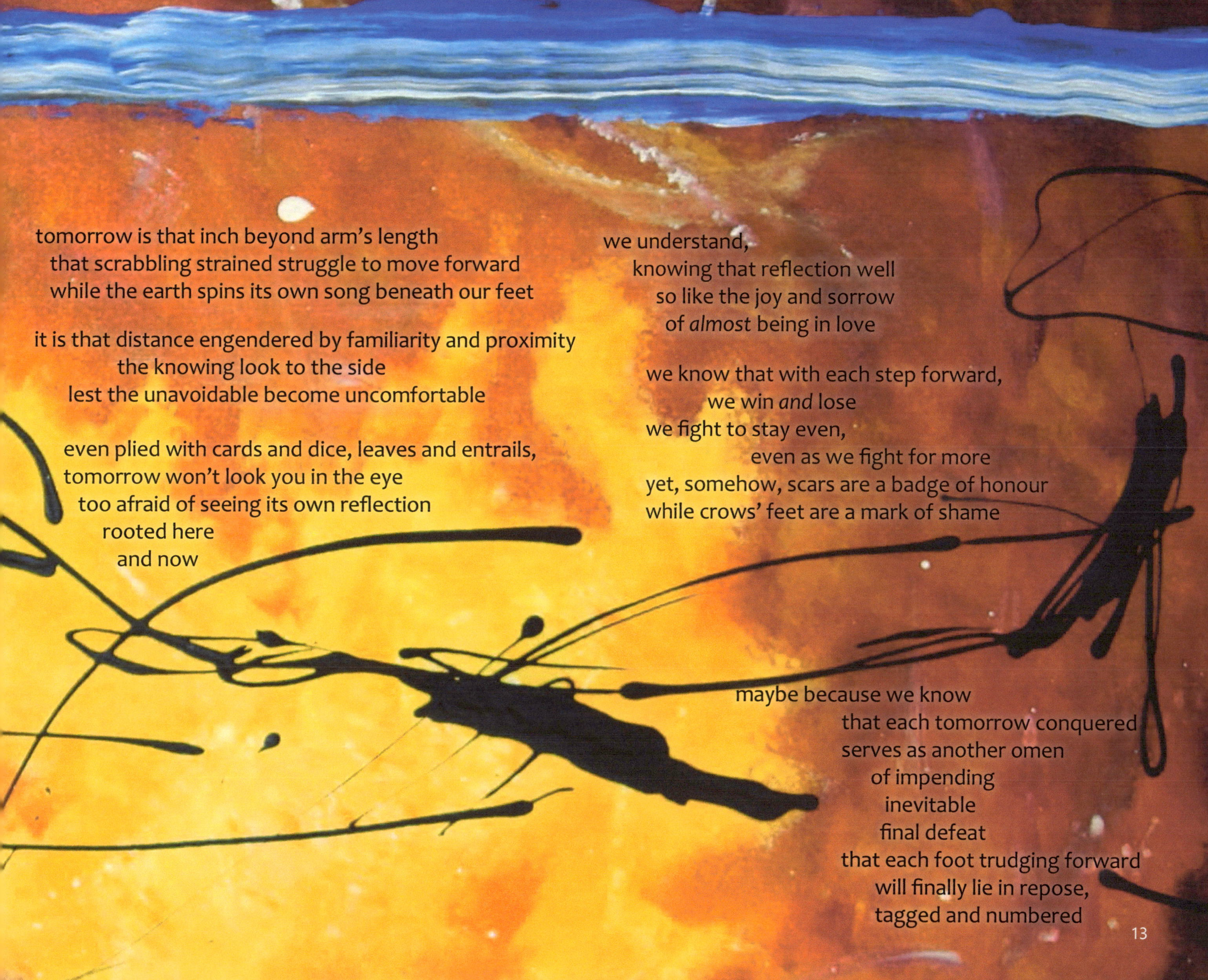

tomorrow is that inch beyond arm's length
  that scrabbling strained struggle to move forward
  while the earth spins its own song beneath our feet

it is that distance engendered by familiarity and proximity
   the knowing look to the side
   lest the unavoidable become uncomfortable

  even plied with cards and dice, leaves and entrails,
  tomorrow won't look you in the eye
   too afraid of seeing its own reflection
    rooted here
    and now

we understand,
  knowing that reflection well
   so like the joy and sorrow
   of *almost* being in love

we know that with each step forward,
   we win *and* lose
we fight to stay even,
    even as we fight for more
yet, somehow, scars are a badge of honour
while crows' feet are a mark of shame

    maybe because we know
     that each tomorrow conquered
     serves as another omen
      of impending
       inevitable
       final defeat
     that each foot trudging forward
      will finally lie in repose,
      tagged and numbered

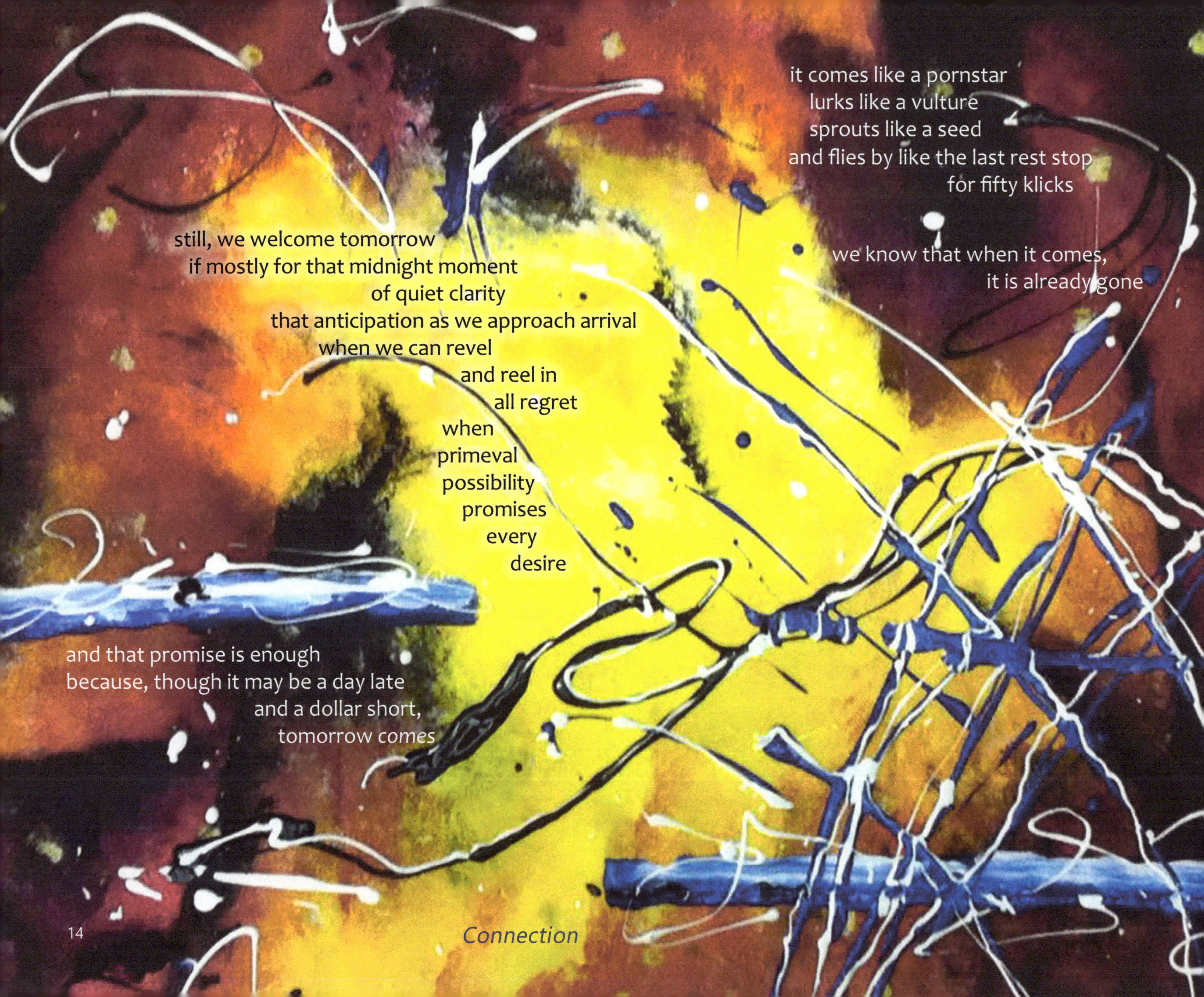

it comes like a pornstar
lurks like a vulture
sprouts like a seed
and flies by like the last rest stop
for fifty klicks

we know that when it comes,
it is already gone

still, we welcome tomorrow
if mostly for that midnight moment
of quiet clarity
that anticipation as we approach arrival
when we can revel
and reel in
all regret
when
primeval
possibility
promises
every
desire

and that promise is enough
because, though it may be a day late
and a dollar short,
tomorrow comes

Connection

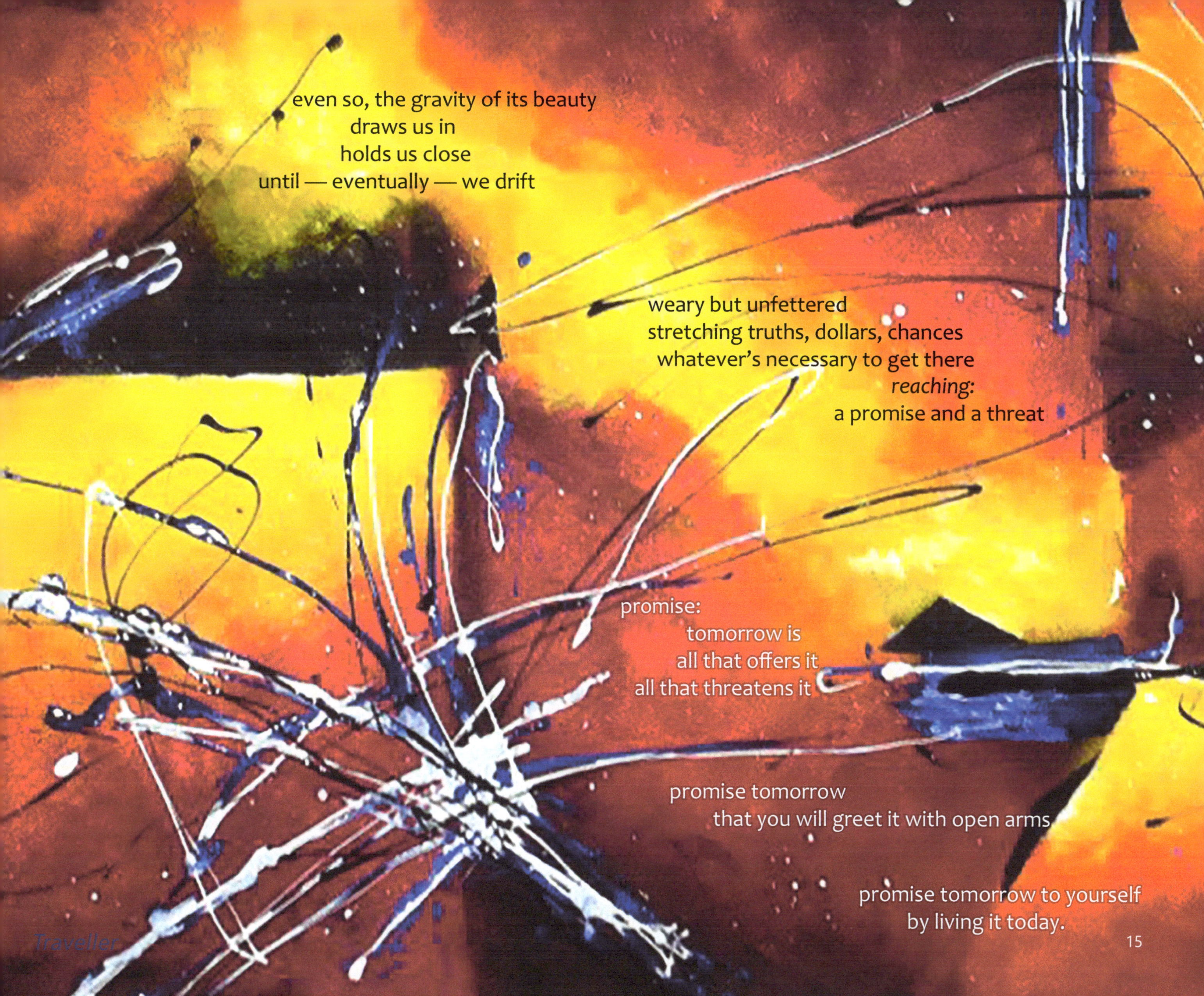

even so, the gravity of its beauty
draws us in
holds us close
until — eventually — we drift

weary but unfettered
stretching truths, dollars, chances
whatever's necessary to get there
reaching:
a promise and a threat

promise:
tomorrow is
all that offers it
all that threatens it

promise tomorrow
that you will greet it with open arms

promise tomorrow to yourself
by living it today.

Traveller

15

some run deep

read like a turkish coffee cup
our past tells our future

our scars tell stories
the bruises & blemishes are moving pictures
frame after frame
of stacked stillnesses
projected outwards

we walk with the weight of such stories
telling of
the strength of the load
the depth of the vein
the burdens borne
the near-misses
the still-a-triumphs
the discord between muscle and marrow

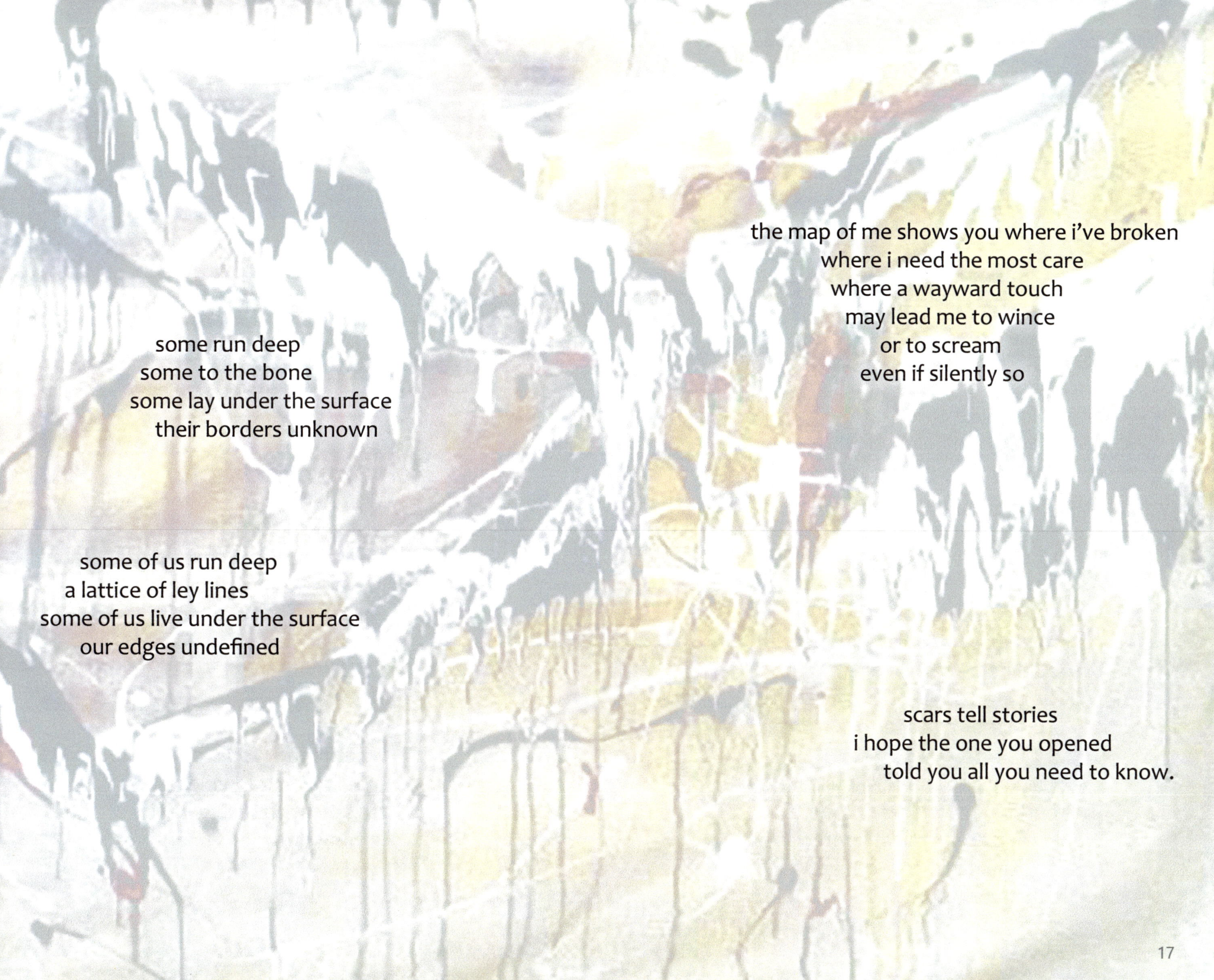

some run deep
some to the bone
some lay under the surface
their borders unknown

the map of me shows you where i've broken
where i need the most care
where a wayward touch
may lead me to wince
or to scream
even if silently so

some of us run deep
a lattice of ley lines
some of us live under the surface
our edges undefined

scars tell stories
i hope the one you opened
told you all you need to know.

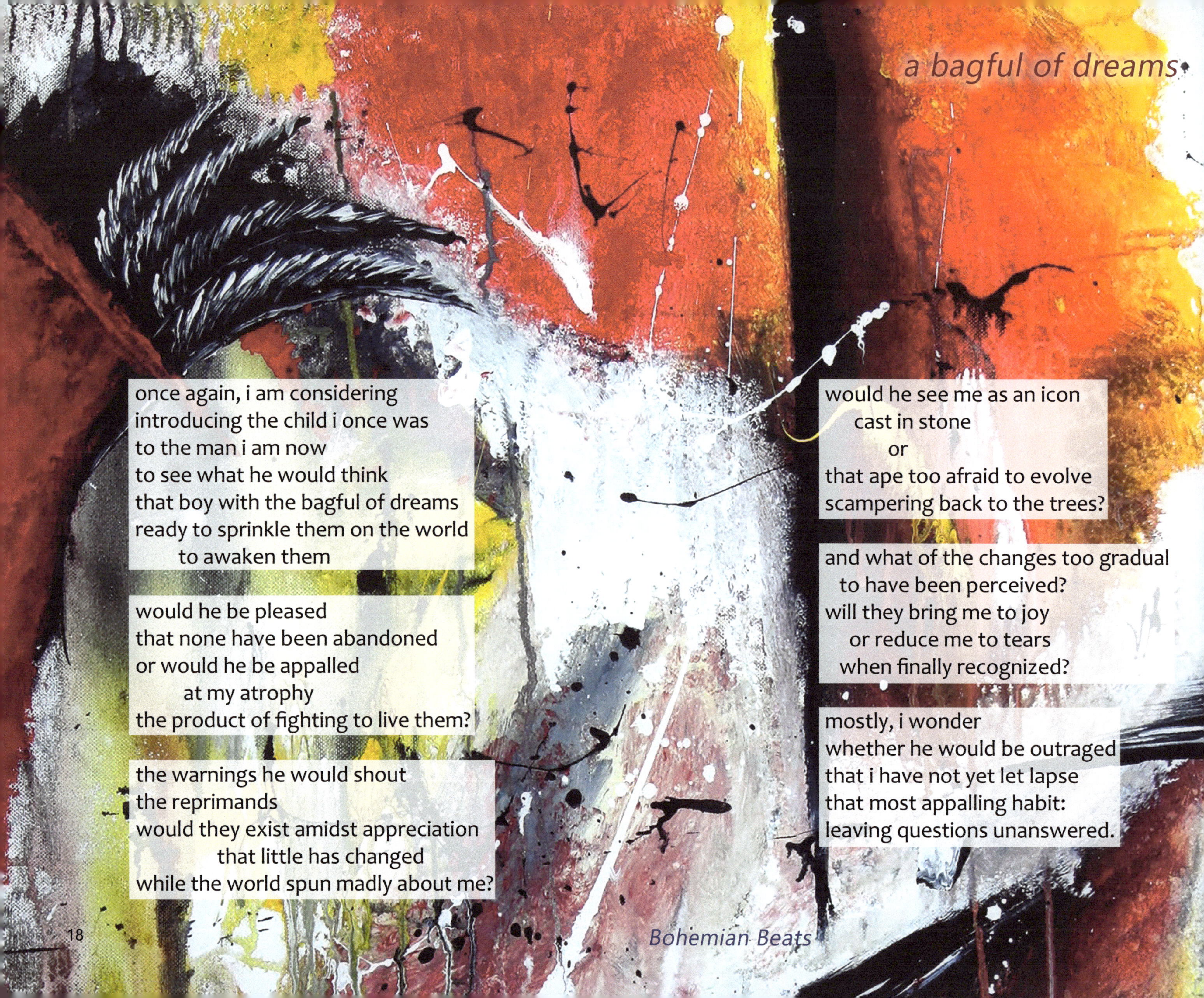

once again, i am considering
introducing the child i once was
to the man i am now
to see what he would think
that boy with the bagful of dreams
ready to sprinkle them on the world
        to awaken them

would he be pleased
that none have been abandoned
or would he be appalled
        at my atrophy
the product of fighting to live them?

the warnings he would shout
the reprimands
would they exist amidst appreciation
        that little has changed
while the world spun madly about me?

would he see me as an icon
    cast in stone
        or
that ape too afraid to evolve
scampering back to the trees?

and what of the changes too gradual
    to have been perceived?
will they bring me to joy
    or reduce me to tears
    when finally recognized?

mostly, i wonder
whether he would be outraged
that i have not yet let lapse
that most appalling habit:
leaving questions unanswered.

amphibious

nothing matters
but that moment
between now and then
between here and there
between will and won't

especially when we know we can be in both

always be amphibious
between the wish you cast into the sea
and the ones you pluck from the air

it's there that you'll find it
whatever you've long been looking for

it's not about what's in your grasp
it's how long you'll let your reach be

extend yourself and maybe
you'll find yourself
inbetween your expectations

or maybe not
because maybe
you've never left yourself there.

canoe

often, we think ourselves adrift
neither recognizing nor revelling
that we still find ourselves
above the waterline

fishing

you will find it
you know this
as sure as you know
that the waiting is work

something will change
something will come   *waiting*
    if time is sacrificed
    on this altar i am

somehow it shall
somehow it must
    because as is
    is not yet enough

    life and nature
        build themselves in change
            and movement
    so standing still
    will eventually get me
        someplace else

that sallow second where thought becomes action
    — well, it can wait a moment
in the now, i'm waiting on the next instant
with its promise of difference from this one

now can feel so heavy
only in later is there the hope of further lightness
something to change
something to come

    adopting the stillness
        practiced by predators
        must lead to reward
        must bring on the difference
            i've been waiting for

        and if not,
        at least biding my time
        keeps me sheltered from blame.

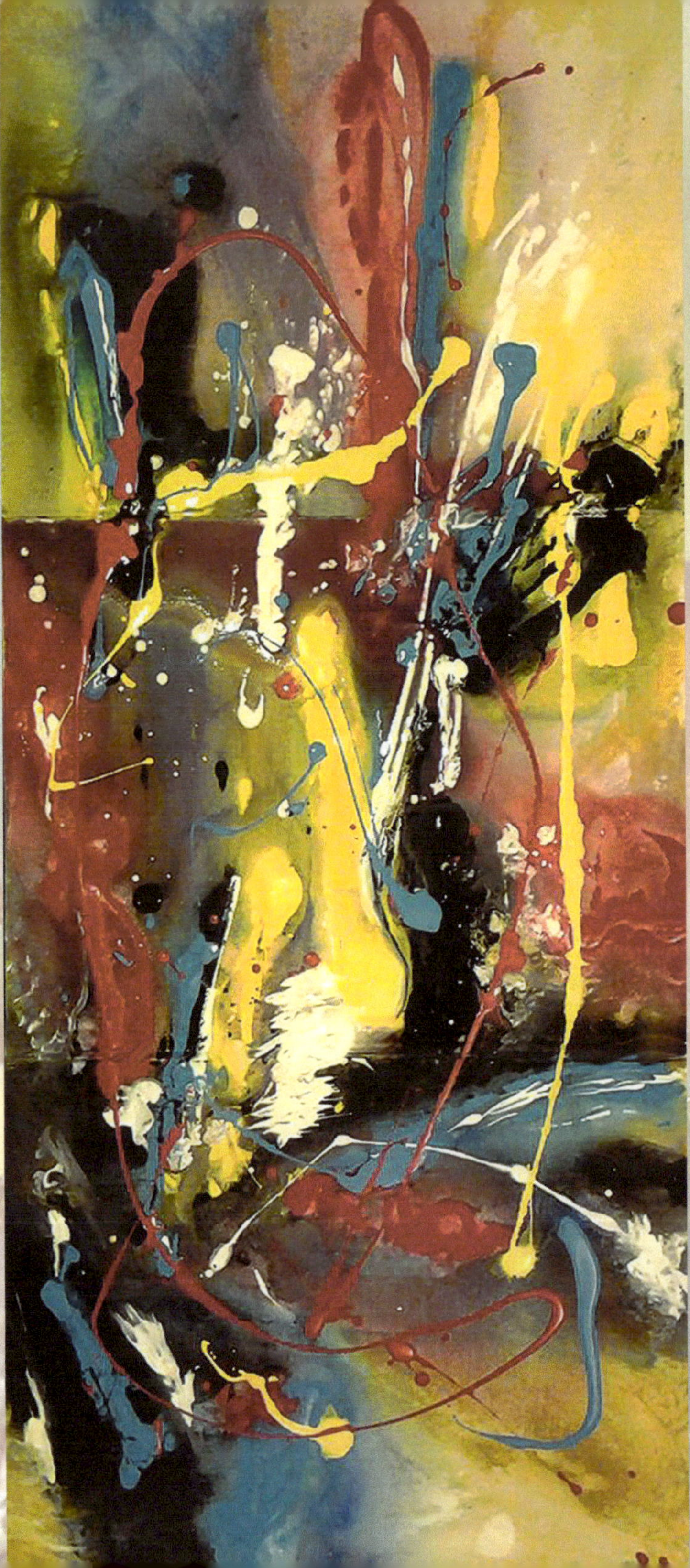

Excitement

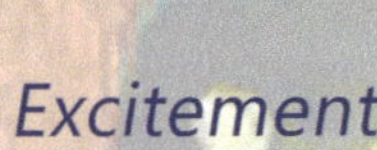

20

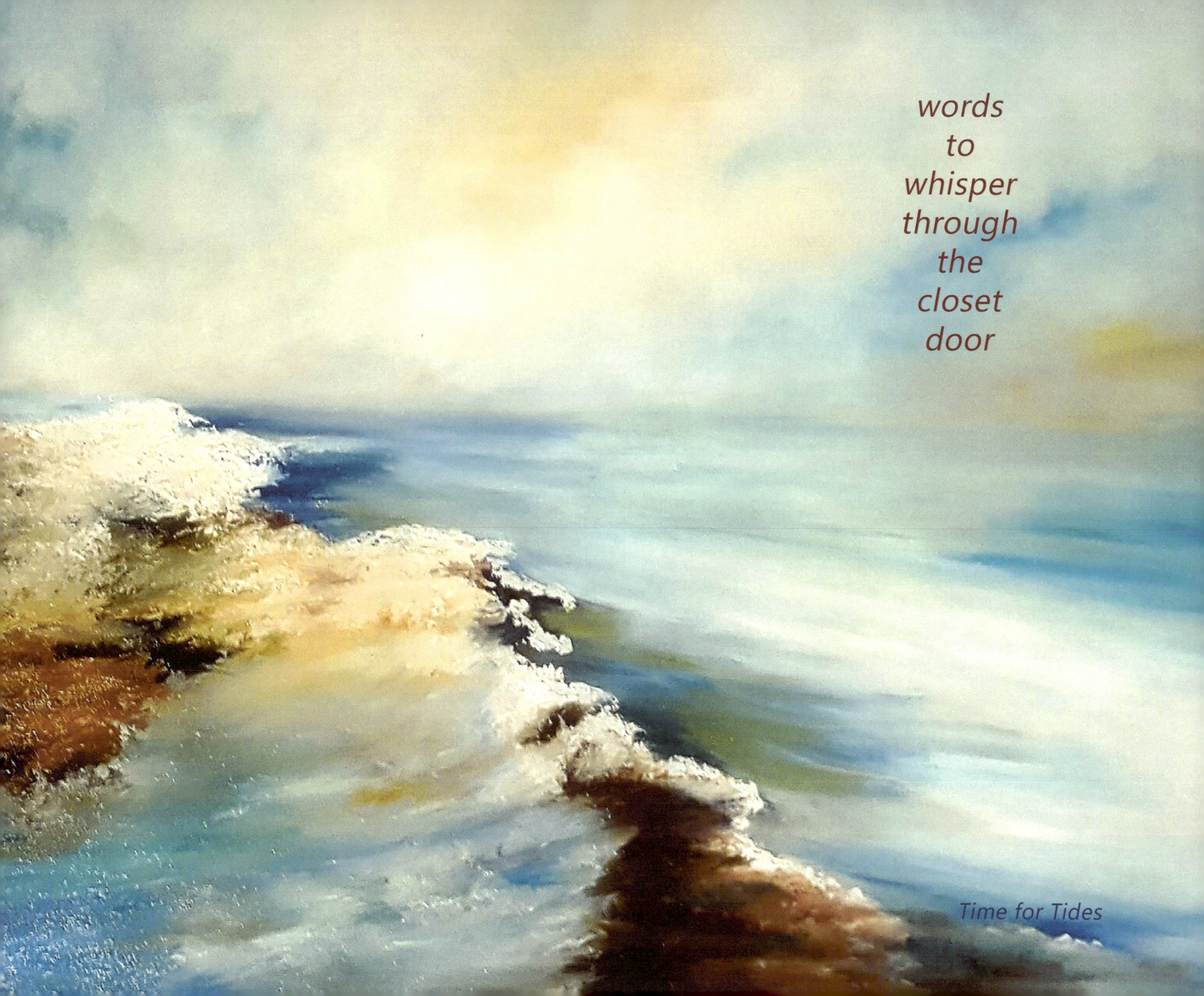

Time for Tides

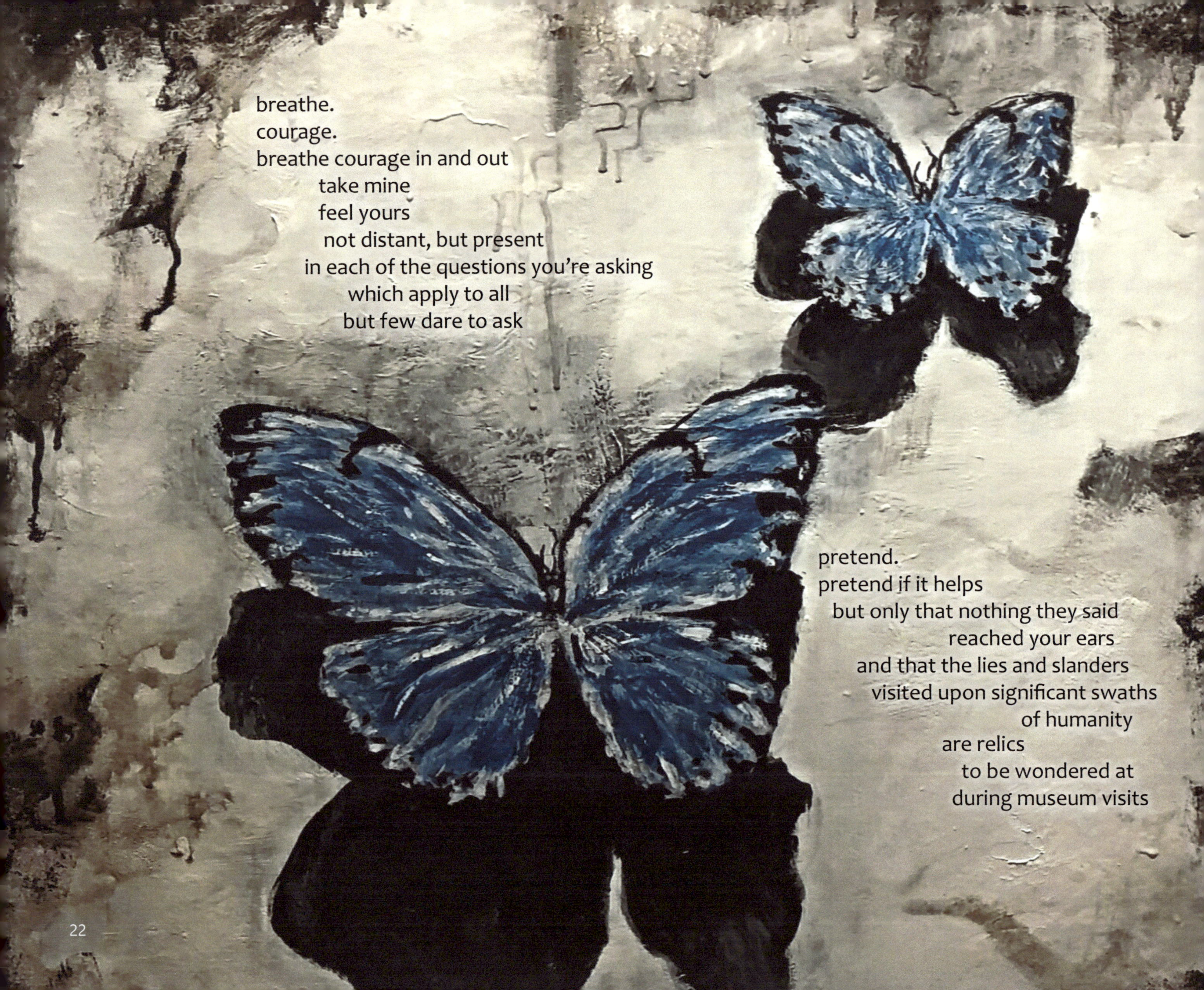

breathe.
courage.
breathe courage in and out
take mine
feel yours
not distant, but present
in each of the questions you're asking
which apply to all
but few dare to ask

pretend.
pretend if it helps
but only that nothing they said
reached your ears
and that the lies and slanders
visited upon significant swaths
of humanity
are relics
to be wondered at
during museum visits

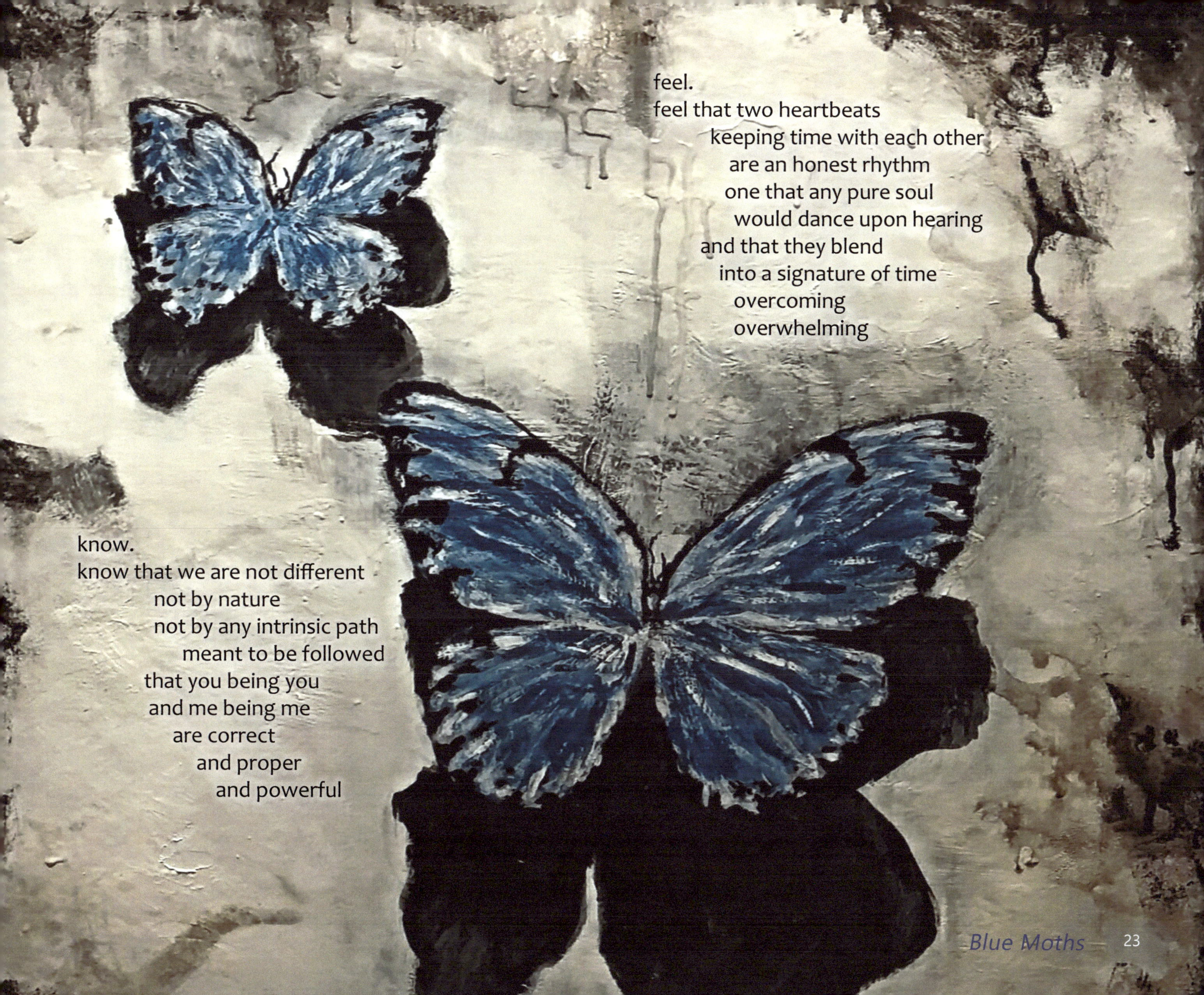

feel.
feel that two heartbeats
        keeping time with each other
        are an honest rhythm
        one that any pure soul
            would dance upon hearing
and that they blend
        into a signature of time
        overcoming
        overwhelming

know.
know that we are not different
        not by nature
        not by any intrinsic path
            meant to be followed
        that you being you
        and me being me
        are correct
            and proper
                and powerful

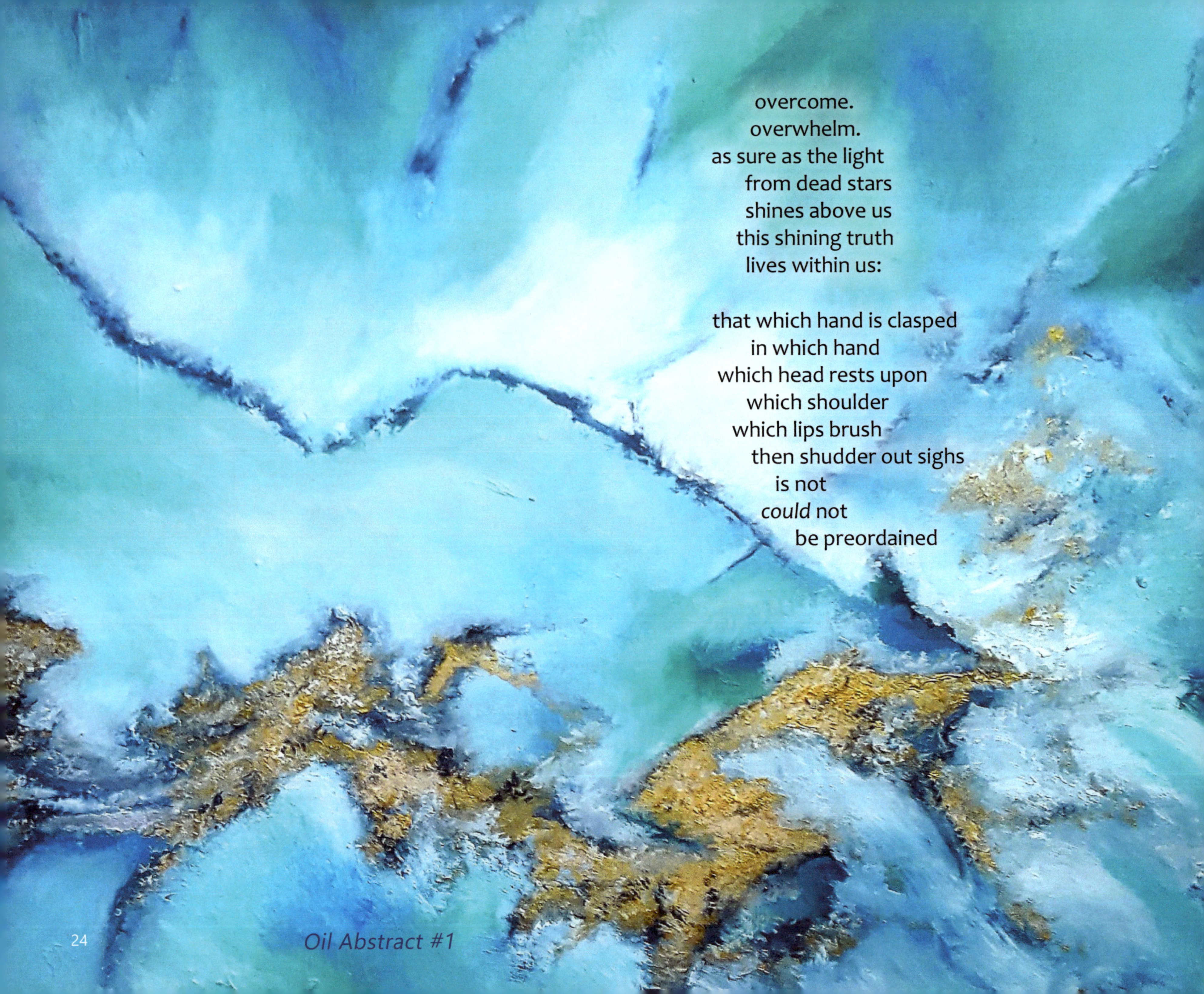

Oil Abstract #1

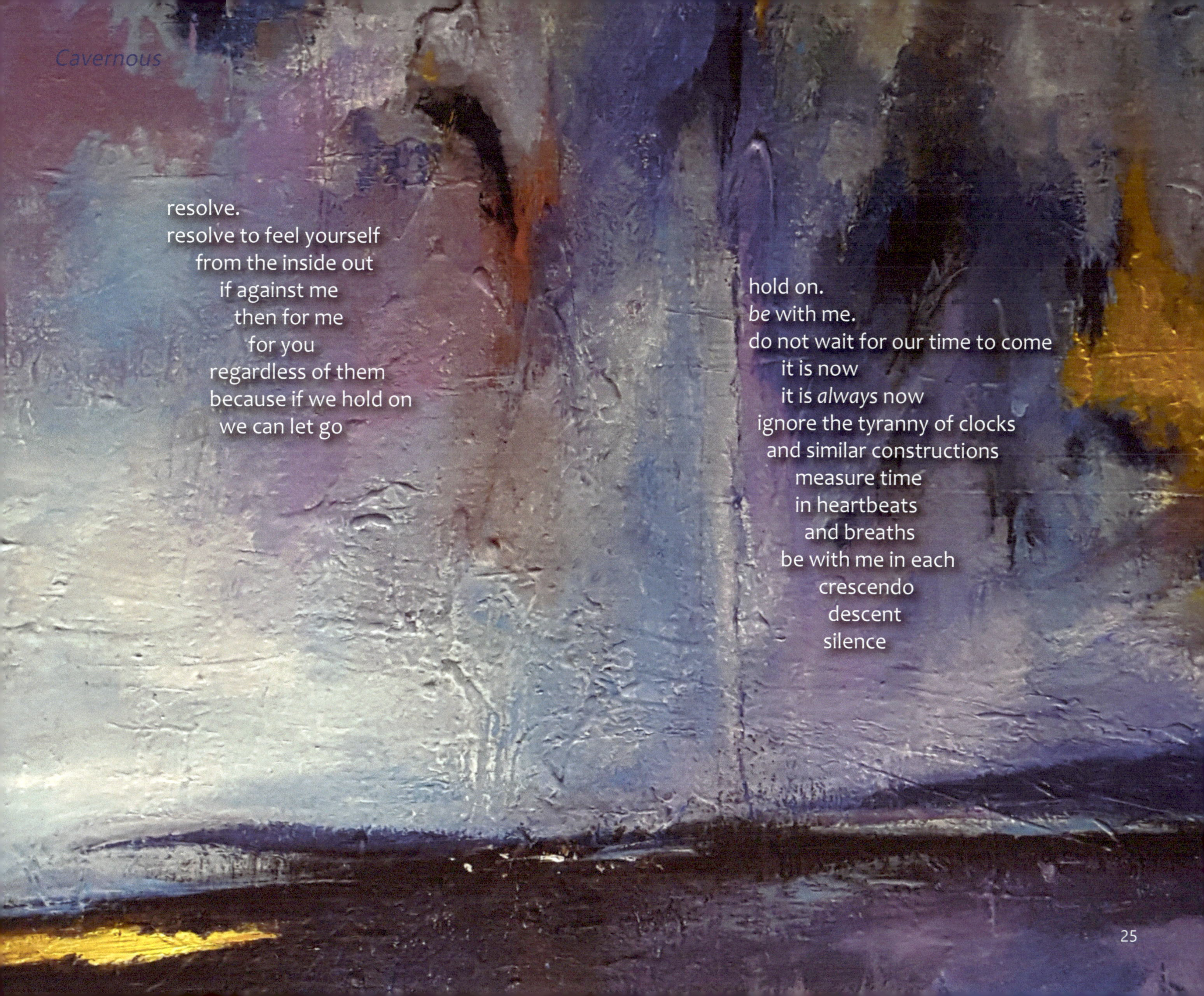
Cavernous

resolve.
resolve to feel yourself
from the inside out
if against me
then for me
for you
regardless of them
because if we hold on
we can let go

hold on.
be with me.
do not wait for our time to come
it is now
it is *always* now
ignore the tyranny of clocks
and similar constructions
measure time
in heartbeats
and breaths
be with me in each
crescendo
descent
silence

let go.
leave it.
leave it to others
     to hang their heads in shame
      or to raise them in wonder
  but give them reason
    by giving yourself freedom

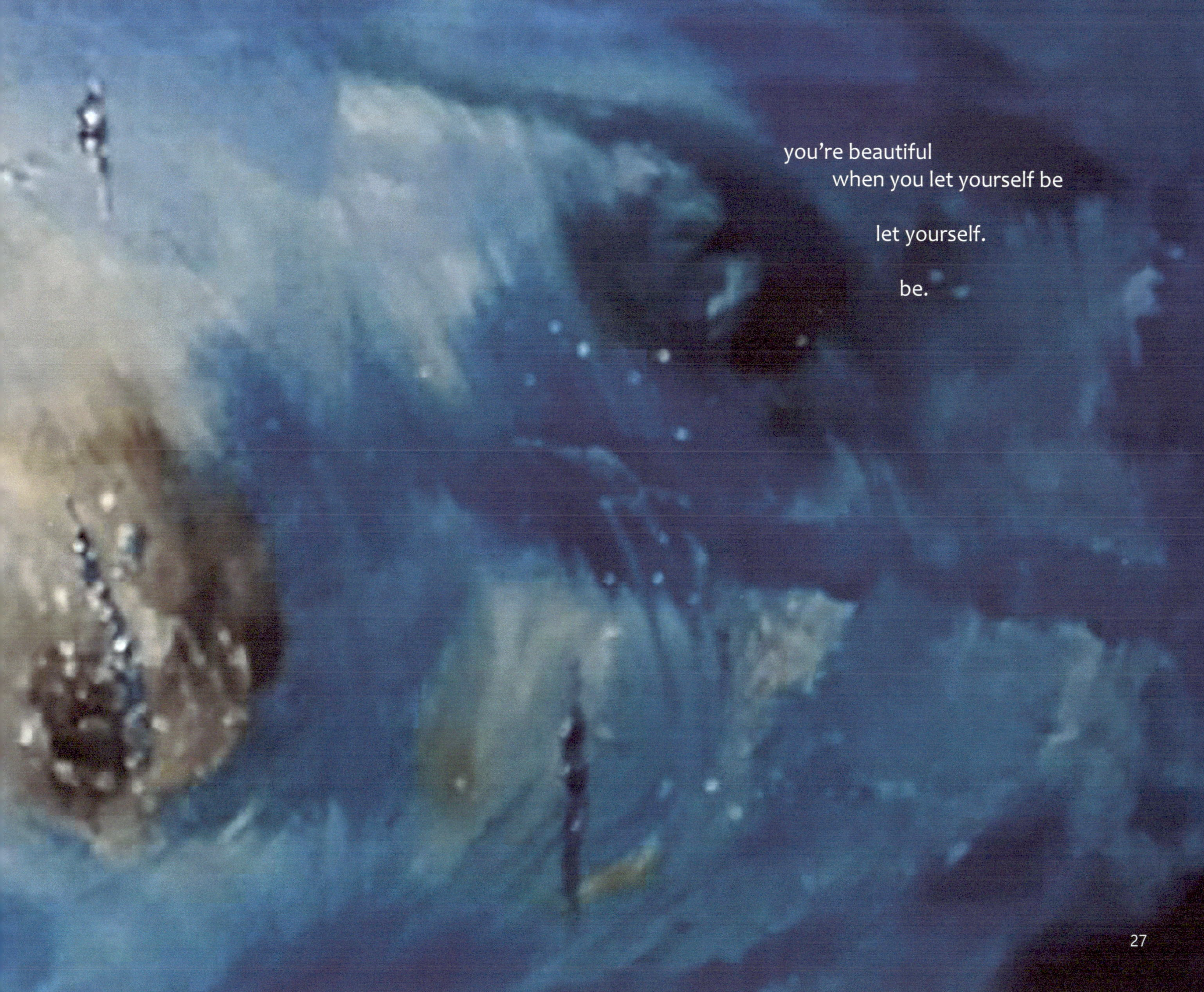
you're beautiful
when you let yourself be

let yourself.

be.

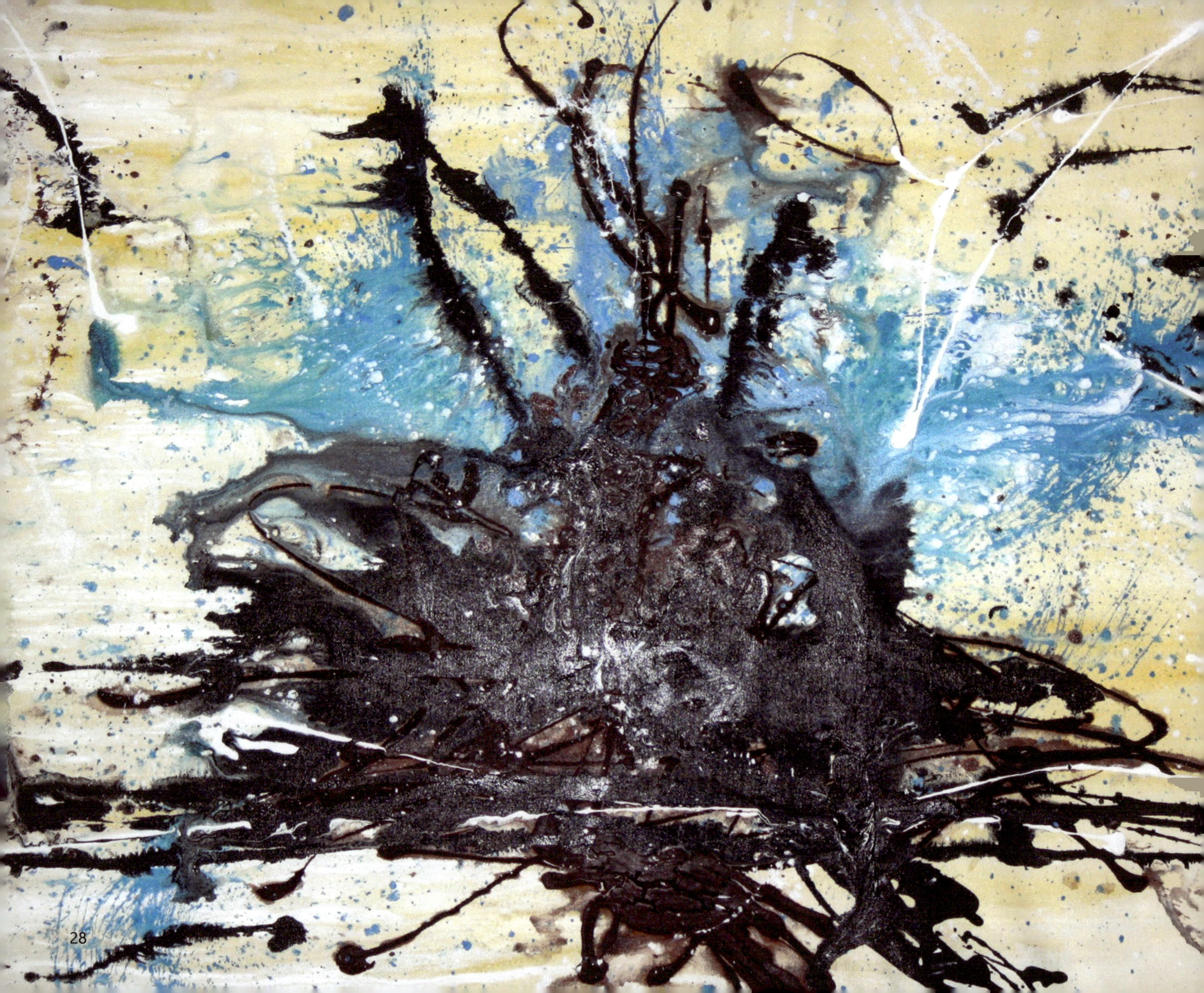

tears in their time

the saddest thing is the readiness
    however necessary we know it is

    the mad dog must be put down
    the drowning man who thrashes left to die
    the bad seed left to rot

necessity wears a harsh and hardened mask
        no matter how sweet and soft
                the face beneath
it *must*
it has no choice
its true face would betray too much
        would not see clearly its task
                through its tears

tears are a luxury in times of need
they wash away resolve
they sting our eyes and blur our vision
they steal the sustenance we need to live

there will be time for crying
        when bellies are full
        when children are safe
        when elders are extolled
        when no hand holds a knife
            other than to slice bread for sharing

there will be time for crying
        though that time will call for tears of joy
            the salt and water of life
            flowing freely between us
                shared as sacraments
exalted as the sacred things they are

there will be time for crying
    after we have found our way through the fire
    after we have burned away
            the excesses and otherness
    after we allow that our edges extend
            far beyond the reach of our skin

there will be time for crying
        for now, be strong
            be ready
            be one
            and become.

out and in

there is out

    and there is in

as arbitrary as
    the separation between them may be
we do not spend our days in doorways
    even when the earthquake threatens
we understand portals to be transitory
we move through them with speed
    lest they close around us
we do not want to be in-between
and heap scorn on the idea of a life in limbo

    what is out
        will come in
    and what is in
        will break out

there are always cracks and breaks to be exploited
    gaps in the lines and definitions
        we'd thought we'd cemented
any contractor can tell you that no seal is perfect
time will whittle away at everything
    it is the universal solvent
        rotting away any barrier we build

we can try to enforce the separation
but we know it will never hold
and we feel that inside

eventually, if we go in
    we know we need to go out
the amphibious drive behind our nature
    prevents either from being enough
the continuous thriving of all things
    requires movement
and any shift will lead eventually
    from one state to another

every entryway is a hole
so why would the opposite not hold true?
ingress is always inviting
    and escape is always enticing
if you don't believe so
    see how long you can keep your mouth shut

that whisper of the wind
        leaking into your living room
inevitable insects and recalcitrant rodents
condensation, moisture, and fog
that scraggly weed sprouting
        where the asphalt gave way
those words you never meant to say
that thought you'd thought had been thrown away

        these will get in
        these will leak out

every boundary will someday give way
so hedging your bets on building walls
        is futile
        and foolish
trying to turn the tide of the transitory
        is a waste of your days
better to open the gates
    and let all flow in either direction

accept the ability to access any of it
affirm that anything can access you

welcome it all in
let it all out
        and know
            that the open doorway is the key.

nothing and no one

castles in the air are bound to fall
those on the ground will decay or be razed
   and no one wants to know

still, you must tell the builders
   shout it into their ears
     as they cement each stone into its place
and whisper it to their orphans
   however cruel it seems

because legacies outlast any layer that might be laid
   and as those tumble or crumble or give
   what lay behind them all is exposed

when we weep for the walls alone
we strip them of meaning
we hold fast to dust returning to dust
rather than to the spark which let it live

   in doing so, we reject life itself

and what then would the walls shelter?
   just the trappings and detritus
those things that say
   someone *used* to be here
     — if anyone is left to listen

those artifacts, however accidental
   pretending at meaning
   mean nothing but pretence
nothing compared to those who carved them
nothing compared to those
   who feel them inscribed in their being
nothing without us creating them
   or being created through them

let nothing stop with you
   — for a while
let it find some shade of shelter
 and become something more
let it give itself to the future
 as a full promise to be filled

for the time will come
   when no one stands in your way
   when no one stands in your shadow
   when you are gone
     — *no one* —
   and if nothing remains
   no one will know.

Eruption

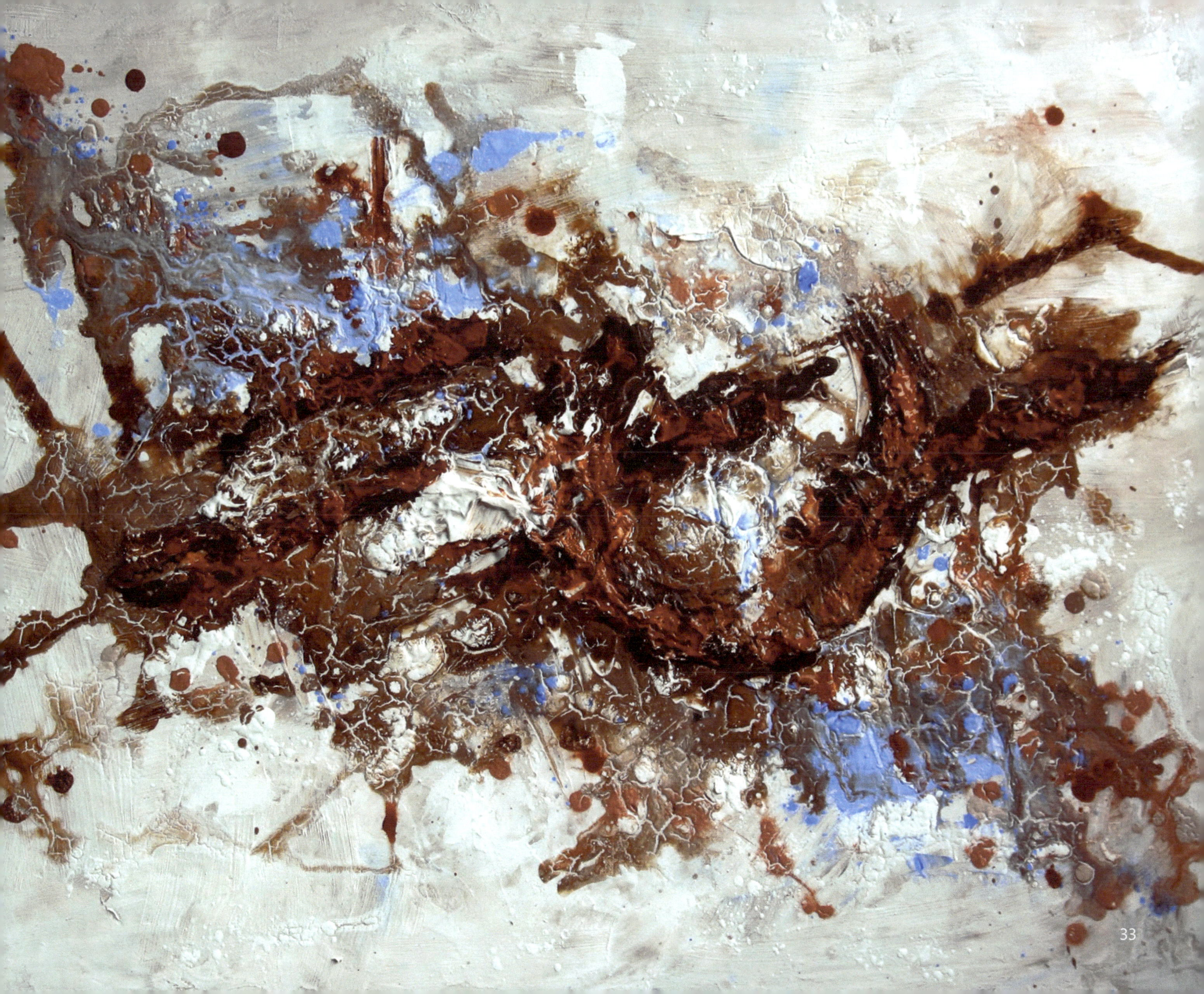

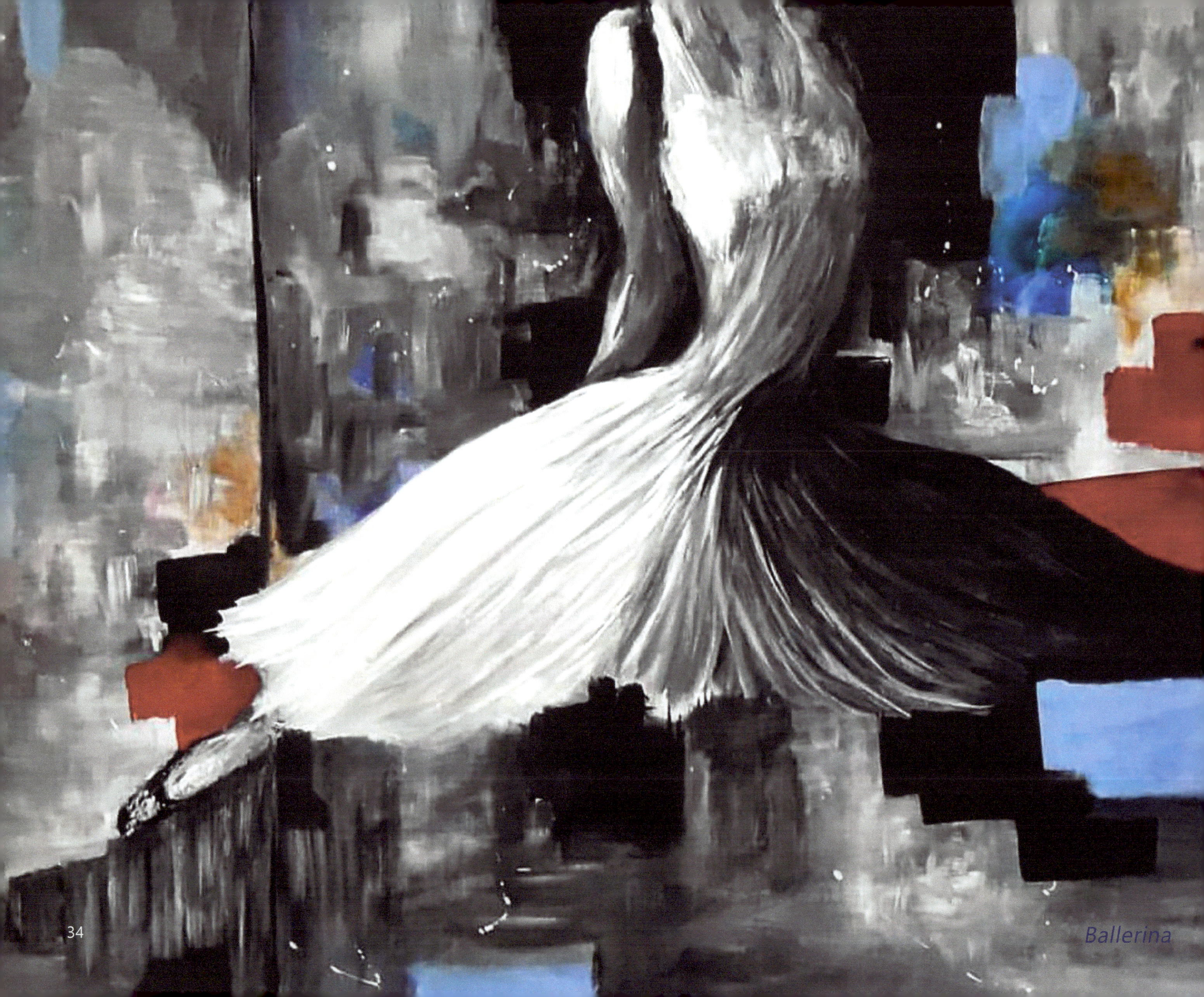

Ballerina

different floors

we work on different floors
but it's the same building

so i'm sharing an elevator with this
      make-believe model and
she thinks she can scrawl her fashion fantasies
      all over
      my mind
      my body
      my libido

        (she's wrong)

   to her, i know how i come off —
   it's written in that sidelong
      skipping-stone glance
that rides quickly up to the floor indicator

to her, i'm just a mystery wrapped in an enigma
wrapped in clothes that aren't from gaulthier
    — with facial hair

   how did she get tangled so tightly
     in that web of wanna-be
   believing paris dictates personality
   that glossy magazines are catalogues of self
   that people mean more
     with other people's names attached

it's not just the fame and glamour —
     she's on a mission
she's a television evangelista
serving up sitcom fantasy
but refusing to hit the fridge
   at the commercial break

she's stereotype —
  self-proclaimed archetype —
    polished,
    practiced,
    precise

not a word,
not a step,
not a move of her own

i can't see anything that's her

  excepting the fear
    each time she turns away

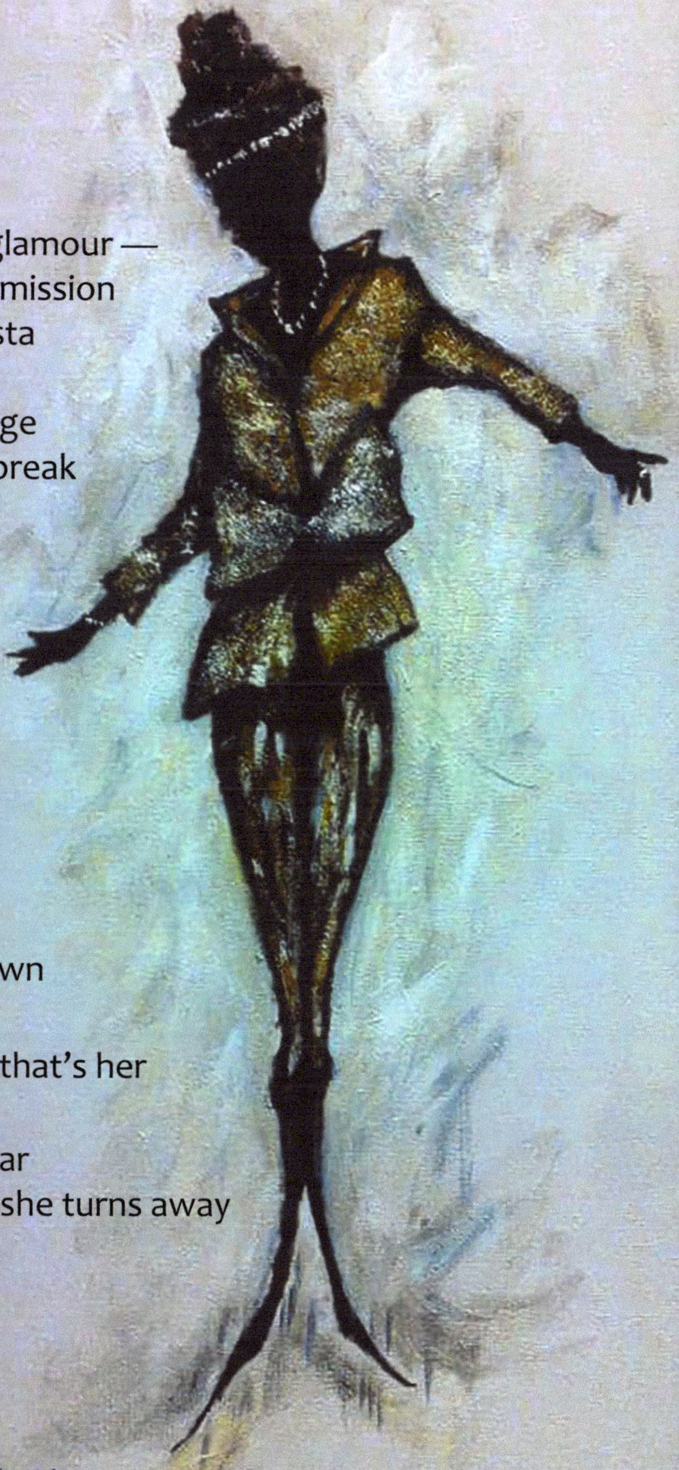

Fashionista

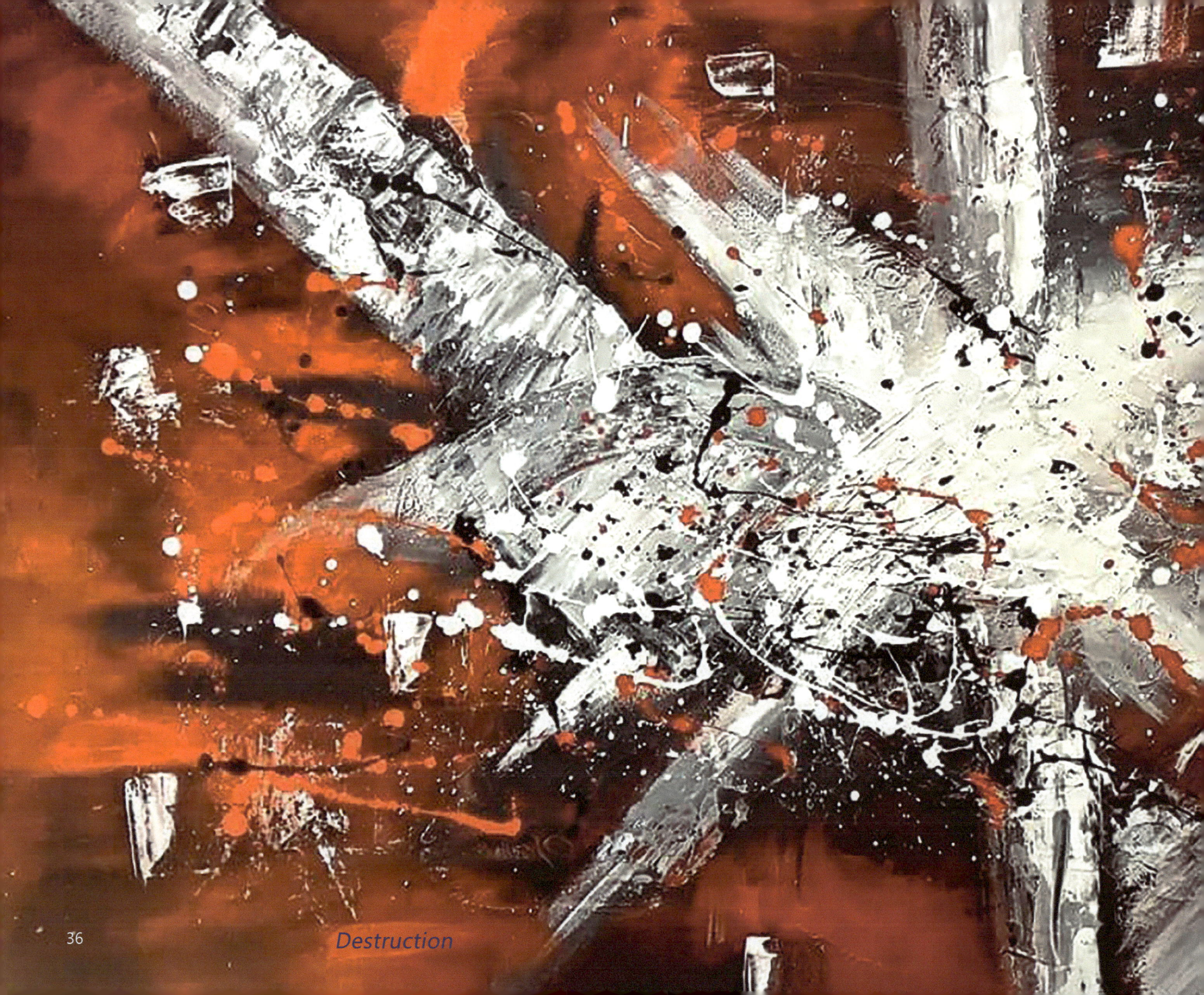

Destruction

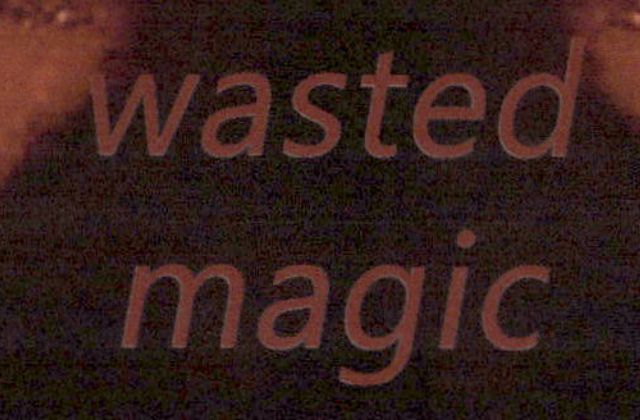

wasted
magic

the problem with love at first sight
  is the second thoughts

because
    though we can lock eyes
    and see who each other is
        in an instant
    only time can tell us
    whether we're willing to live up to that

perhaps those perfect people
        as first spotted
    unblemished by the scars
        inflicted from outside
could live up to that promise of passion

perhaps they,
        undaunted by the daily drudgeries
        of fears steering us in circles
        could stand up strong
            and surrender

maybe it's in that moment
    four opened eyes
    dilating to let the light in
    that the shadows disappear

        maybe it's the mirroring
        seeing ourselves shown
        as reflection
        on another's part
        which reminds us to re-emerge

surely, the exchanged glance
    photons flying a beeline
    passing through each other
    to illuminate connections
    this transcendent science
        is reduced
        to wasted magic

when we allow the mundane
to break the spell

why do we look away?
why do we not stare deeper?
    delve to the depths of the soul?

    ask anyone this
    and their gaze will fall
        because we know
        that the fear finds us from within

    it whispers in our ears
    it nudges us away
    it keeps us plodding onward
        without looking back
        until it's too late

Fireflies

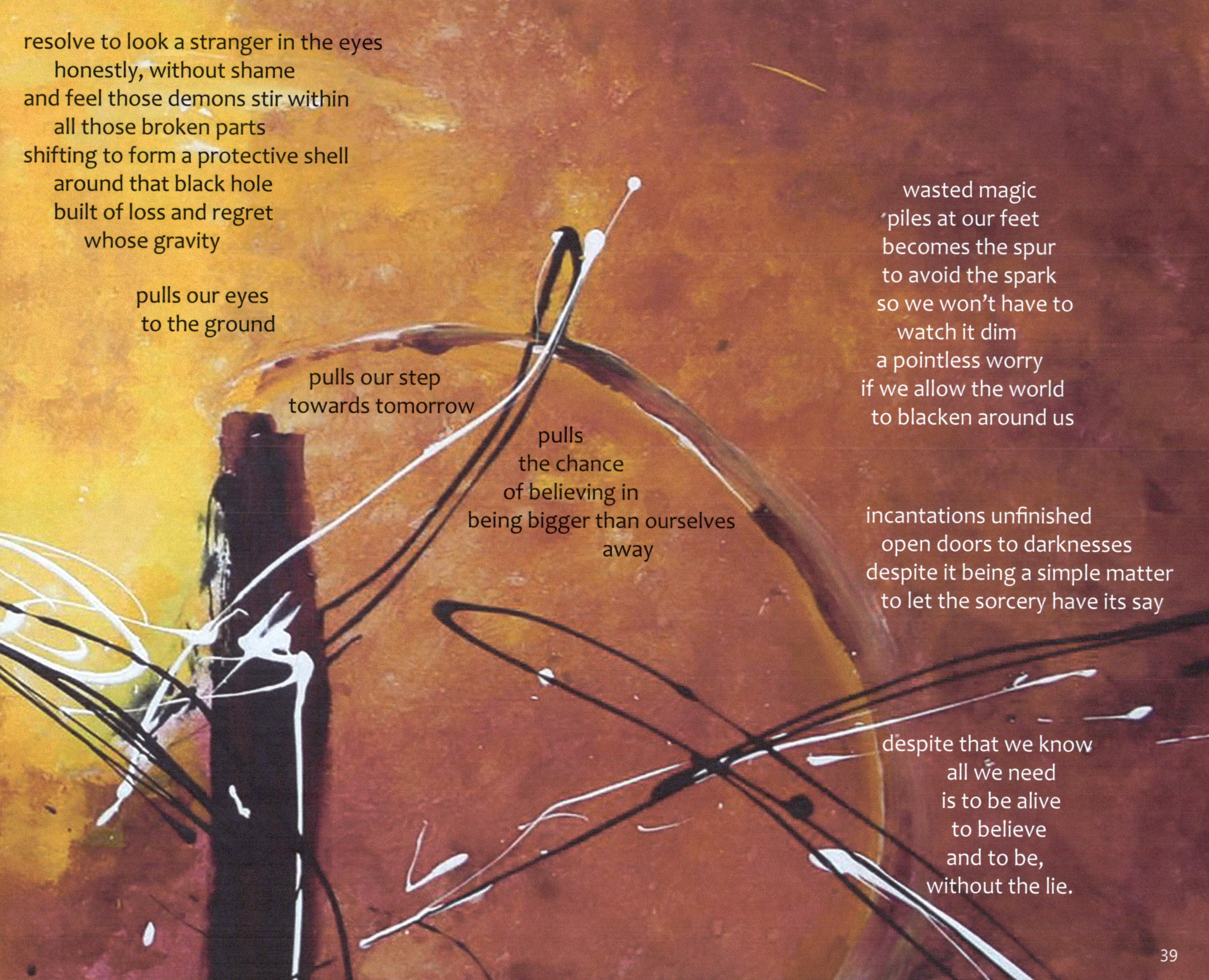

resolve to look a stranger in the eyes
   honestly, without shame
and feel those demons stir within
   all those broken parts
shifting to form a protective shell
   around that black hole
   built of loss and regret
    whose gravity

    pulls our eyes
     to the ground

    pulls our step
towards tomorrow

    pulls
    the chance
   of believing in
being bigger than ourselves
    away

wasted magic
piles at our feet
becomes the spur
to avoid the spark
so we won't have to
watch it dim
a pointless worry
if we allow the world
to blacken around us

incantations unfinished
open doors to darknesses
despite it being a simple matter
to let the sorcery have its say

despite that we know
all we need
is to be alive
to believe
and to be,
without the lie.

39

the opposite of fear

the opposite of fear
    is the fingers of two hands entwining
        in knowledge of each other

the opposite of fear
    is an accidental brush in passing
        that evokes a smile

the opposite of fear
    is a distant whisper
        understood by its tone alone

there is safety in most things
                that bring comfort
        but not love
        love is a minefield
    where each successful step
    is rewarded with exhilaration
    as the heart quickens
    knowing all is risked at every moment

as such, it cannot be given lightly
    hold fast to it
love is not meant for cowards
and your strength shows
when you look it in the eye
    — honestly —
    because truth is bravery
    and lies at its foundation

and it
    is our foundation
our stories
    our histories
        our fictions
            our songs
    these dance on the bedrock of love
        they rise from it
in majestic structures like the taj mahal

        we want to rise
we want to be greater than one
        because we know we are

            we know
        we are not solitary
        we are not alone
        we are not bound by
        the borders of our bodies

Lynn Canyon
Suspension Bridge

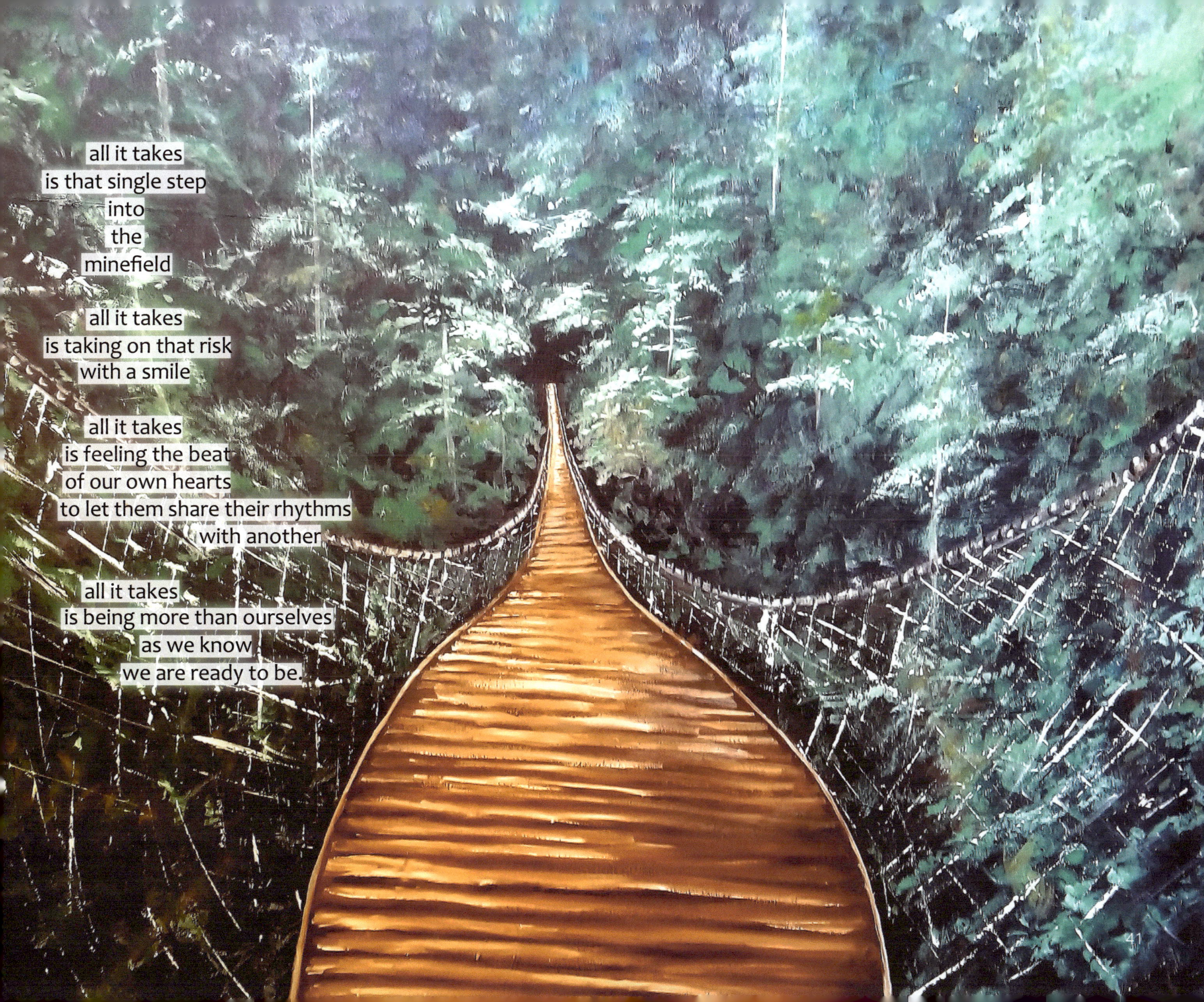
all it takes
is that single step
into
the
minefield

all it takes
is taking on that risk
with a smile

all it takes
is feeling the beat
of our own hearts
to let them share their rhythms
with another

all it takes
is being more than ourselves
as we know
we are ready to be.

straight white male

friends of mine have been hit hard
by a dynamic expressed generally in generalities
they're dismissed in a stroke
by virtue of their race, gender, and sexuality

in fact, i've seen many so cowed
that they've even joined in

i find myself unable to hold back any longer
so i am here to plead to you today
in defence of the straight white male

one stereotype perpetuates another
and so i ask you, one and all
to reconsider this figure

pity these poor creatures
for ages now, most have suffered from a lack
of strong, empowered women in their lives
of the wisdom of innumerable cultures
of reason to redefine their sexuality and gender
— on their own terms

they have no mohandas gandhi
no martin luther king
no laura secord
no chief seattle
no oscar wilde
no george sands
no billie holiday
no boodica

ask yourself whether the will of the majority
is something you'd ever want ascribed to yourself
or if you could ever truly learn history
if it meant bearing the weight of its guilt

how much harder must it be
to expand your horizons
when only given the breadth
of being the defining point
for butch
or tanned
or queer?

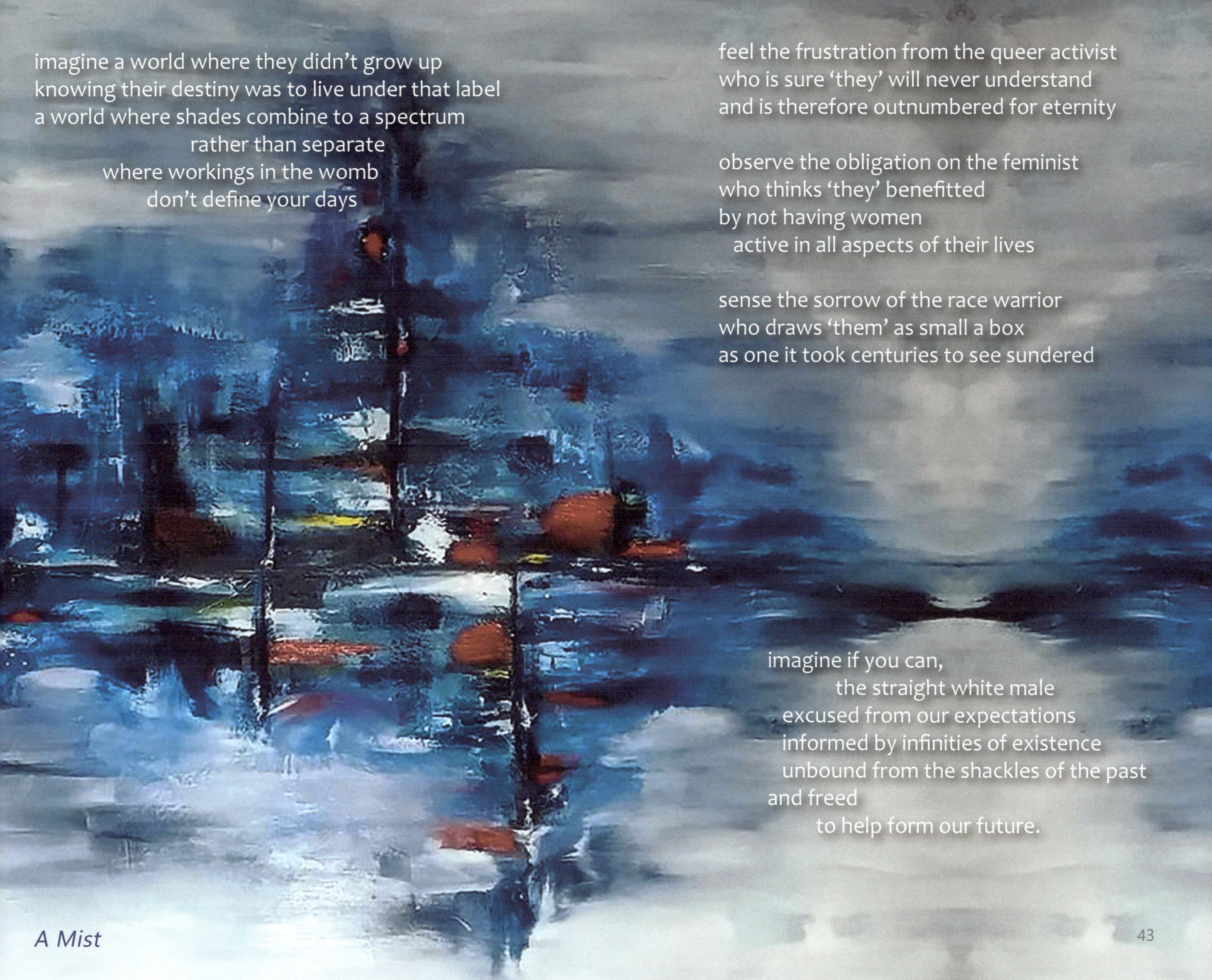

imagine a world where they didn't grow up
knowing their destiny was to live under that label
a world where shades combine to a spectrum
                rather than separate
where workings in the womb
        don't define your days

feel the frustration from the queer activist
who is sure 'they' will never understand
and is therefore outnumbered for eternity

observe the obligation on the feminist
who thinks 'they' benefitted
by not having women
   active in all aspects of their lives

sense the sorrow of the race warrior
who draws 'them' as small a box
as one it took centuries to see sundered

imagine if you can,
        the straight white male
     excused from our expectations
     informed by infinities of existence
     unbound from the shackles of the past
and freed
        to help form our future.

A Mist

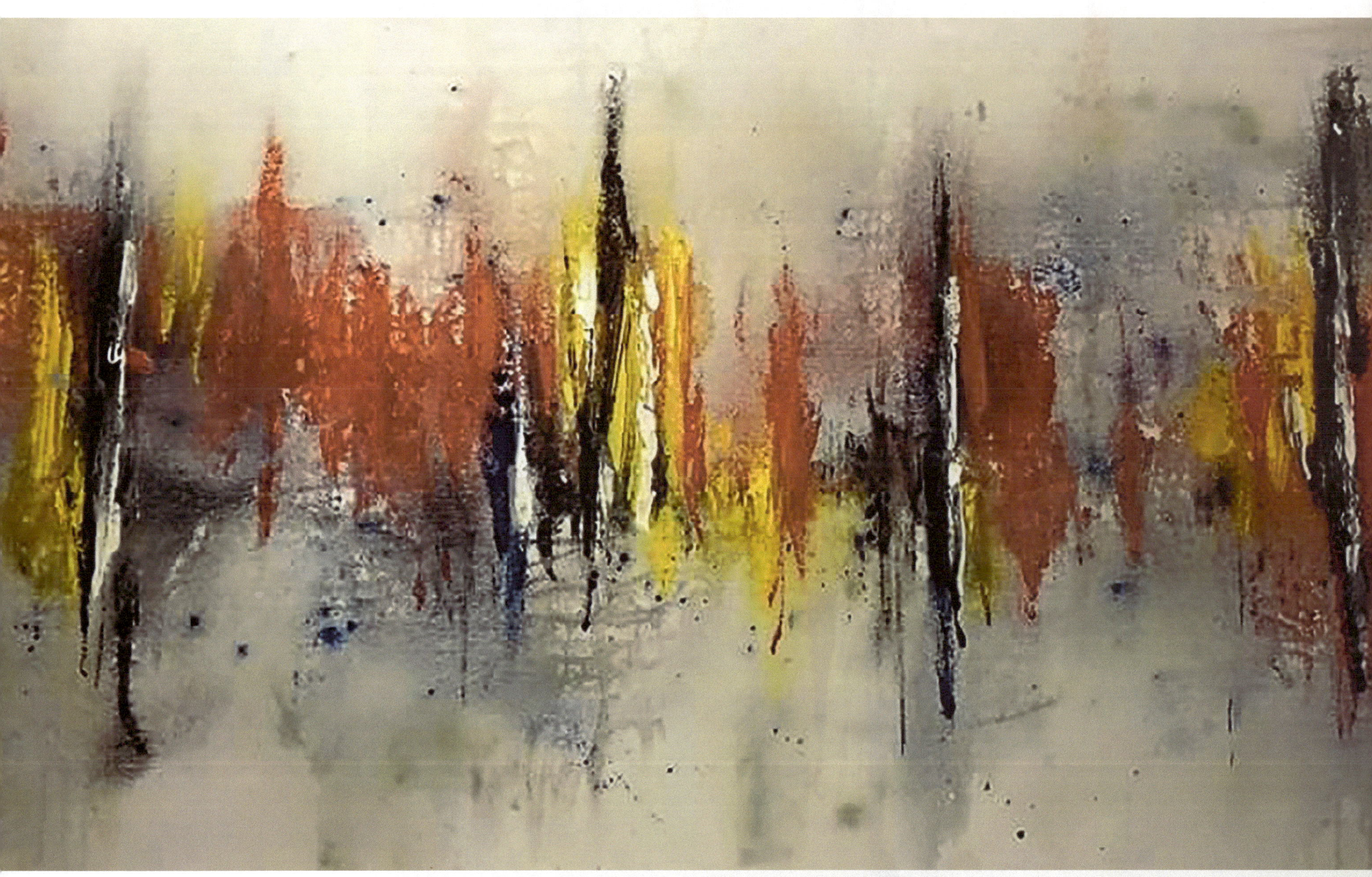

Beats

<h1 style="text-align:center">the duck</h1>

outside the library,
people sit on the steps
   some reading
   some eating
   some smoking
   some taking the sun

a duck
   scrounges for food

on various stairs,
empty stare
  after empty stare
registers
 duck
and nothing more

he approaches me, no fear
plucking at wilted lettuce
one step below my feet
to demonstrate his need

i throw him a look that says
   duck, if i had some...

he shrugs, winks, and continues
going down three steps
before passing the woman parallel
who only takes notice when he slips
                falls

he dives back up
to avoid the two smoking further down
no fear of the cigarette
mine gave him no pause

the duck circles
watching a man eat
a triple-decker jelly sandwich
  while smoking
oblivious that food
looks good to those that hunger

the duck shakes his head
    circles again
running up the upper walkway
chased by a teenage girl
  above her head, cartoon-like
    i see the whole of her thoughts:
      duck!

she leaves
and he settles back beside me
hoping for agreement on the state
  of this motley crew
before pausing to watch a man
  wheel a dog by
  in a shopping cart

the dog is afraid
  — not of the cart —
but of what lies outside
of that small mercy
the duck seems envious

i throw him a look that says
    duck, if i had one...

he seems to snicker and sigh
in a way that says
    if you did, pal,
      i'd ride
    if you did,
      i'd ride.

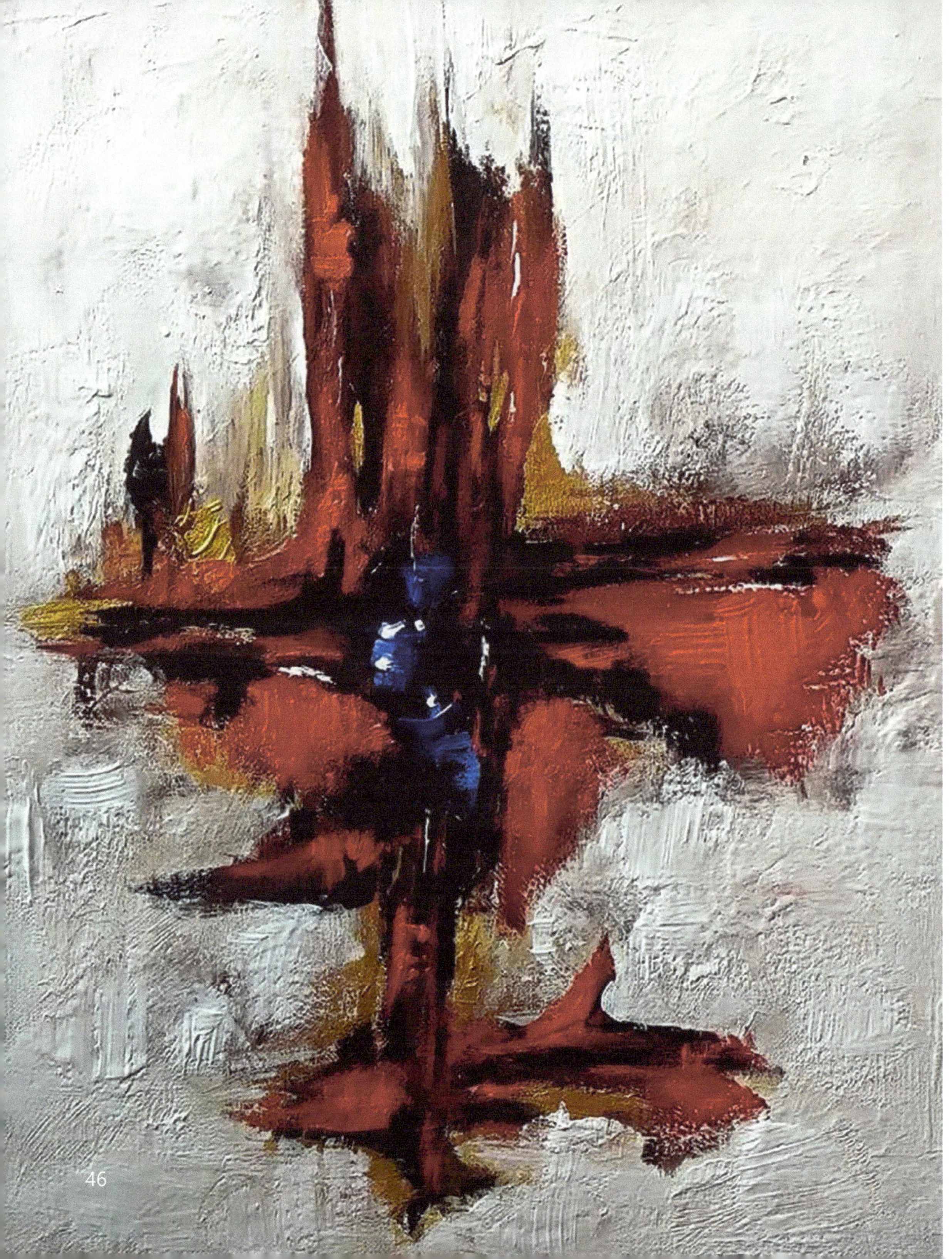

child with a kite

the child with a kite
is sheathed in corona
as the sun blazes down to day's end

a flight of rainbow
cleaves through the blue
and the gulls sing approval

her joy is written across the clouds
and in spray of sand
from wayward feet

she is a silhouette
an unformed memory
of being one with the world

hand clenched on string
she dances between
earth and sky

the rest of us
need only turn and watch
to hear the music
and remember how to fly.

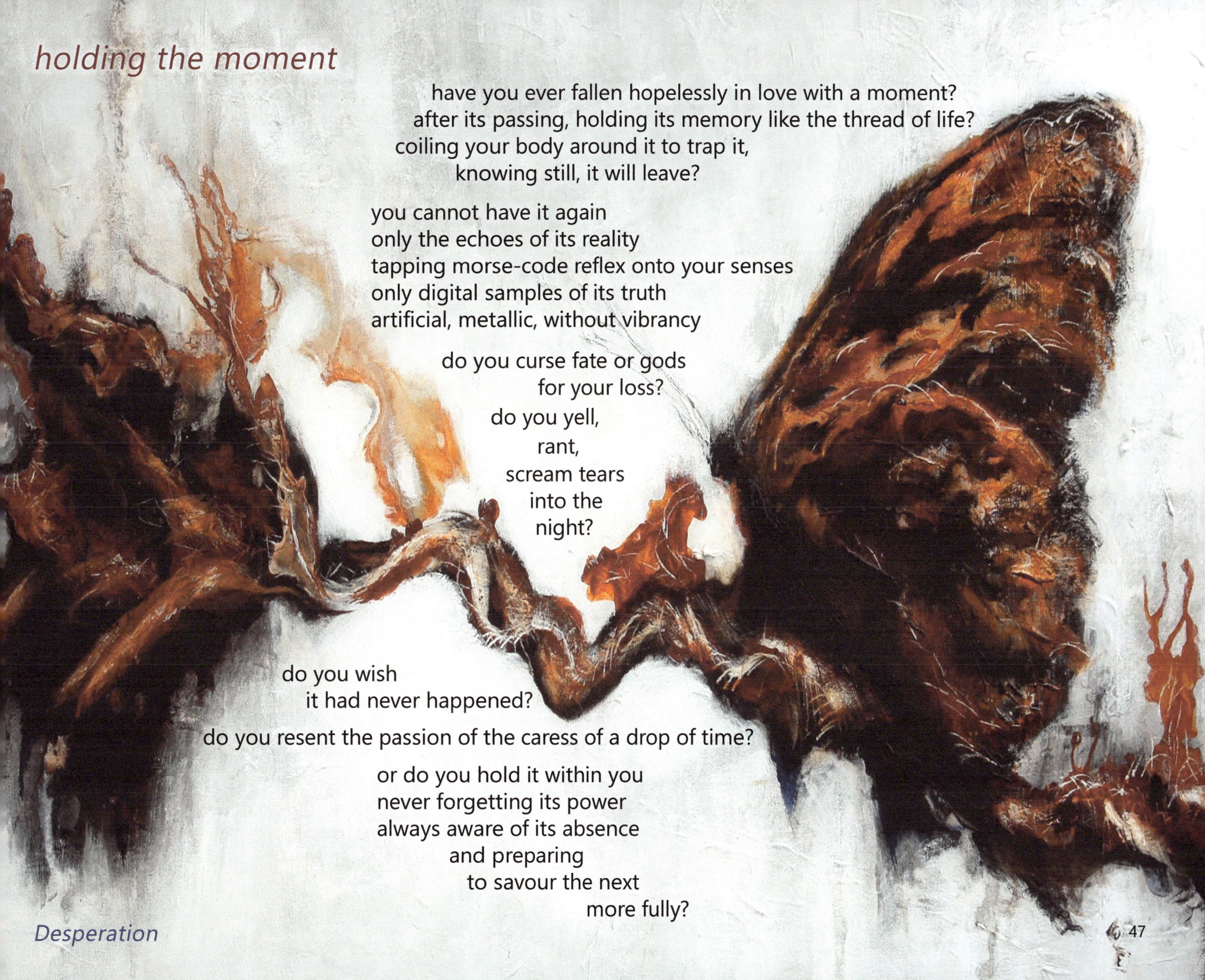

holding the moment

have you ever fallen hopelessly in love with a moment?
after its passing, holding its memory like the thread of life?
coiling your body around it to trap it,
knowing still, it will leave?

you cannot have it again
only the echoes of its reality
tapping morse-code reflex onto your senses
only digital samples of its truth
artificial, metallic, without vibrancy

do you curse fate or gods
for your loss?
do you yell,
rant,
scream tears
into the
night?

do you wish
it had never happened?

do you resent the passion of the caress of a drop of time?

or do you hold it within you
never forgetting its power
always aware of its absence
and preparing
to savour the next
more fully?

Desperation

47

the sweep of time and tide

the tide has a rhythm
    sure, maybe that of the sloppy drummer
    who speeds and slows in the moment
        but it's live, it's living

not like the artificial ticks of the clock
  we pretend is the pace of time
those pointed hands are accusatory
they shift blame in a constant circle

the lapping of waves heals us
    soothes our senses
  while the insistence of the second hand
    we recognize as the sound
     of impending madness

both are sweeping lines
  carrying us forward
maybe to new shores and new days
perhaps from ancient paths and old ways

but we can choose whether our way
       is written
in the curves and bends of welcoming beaches
or in the arrows aiming everywhere but away

the direction suggested by those
    never-resting appendages
      is no greater a distance
than the ocean origin of that whitecap

neither will be reached casually
neither is within our grasp
neither is within a day's journey
   or this side of the skyline

we only see the thin edge of their expanse
but one is always the same
    even as it changes
while the other is infinite variety
    in its repetition

  endless grains swept to distant shores are we
and where we rest defines us only in the moment
    however horizons look upon us
     it is always with a sweeping smile
      and the knowledge
     that tomorrow and yesterday
       look the same on the surface
    despite their myriad variations

time has its own measure
   one far beyond us
but one that riffs to the rhythms around us
   those that pre-date us
   reaching back deep
   those we often forget
when falsely favouring the shallows
   of mechanical meters

we fall out of time
   thinking of those shorelines as remote
   thinking of our actions as driven
   by the grinding of gears and wheels
telling ourselves we don't feel
   the pull and push
   of invisible forces
and letting all our chances tick away.

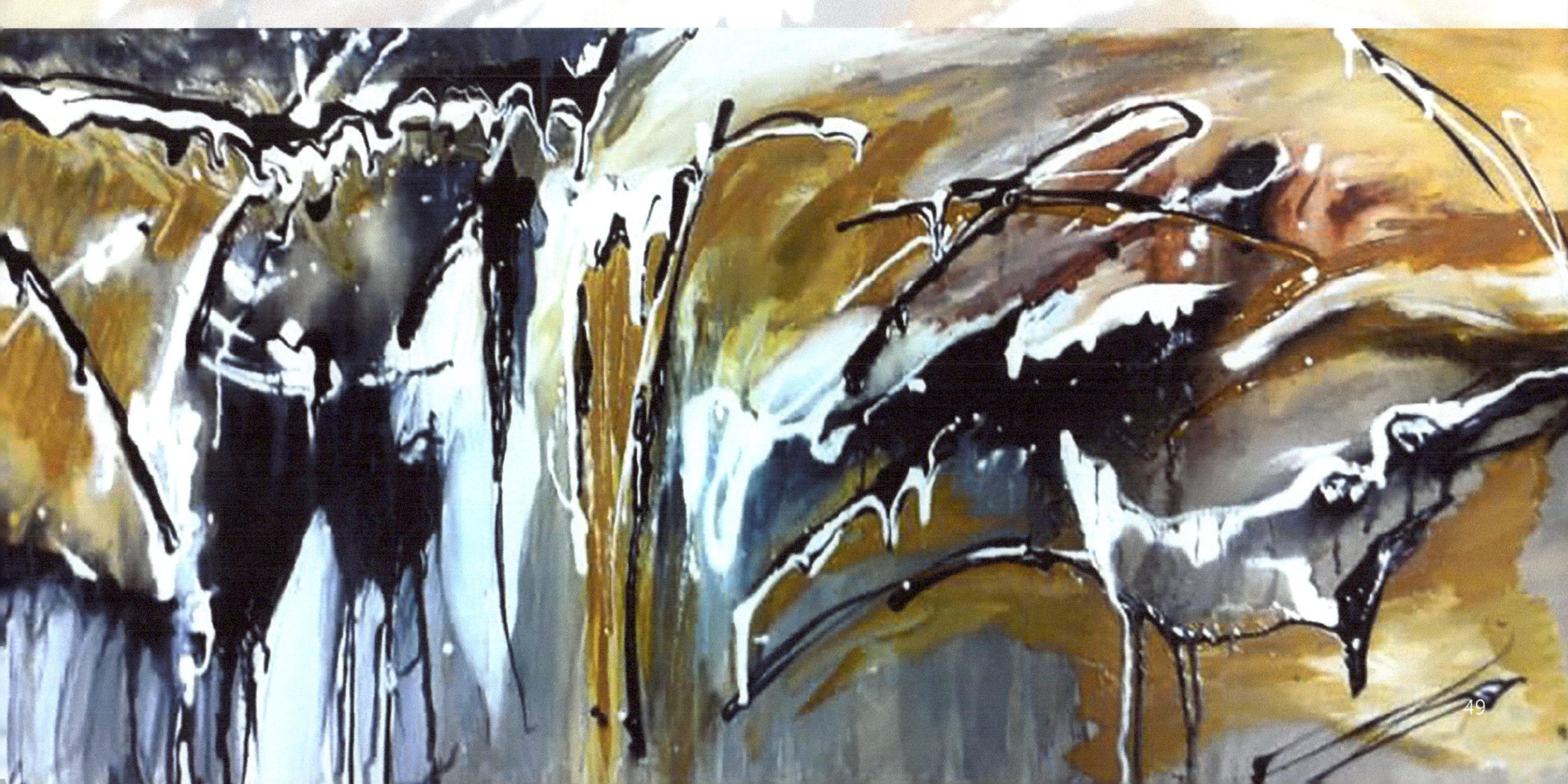

dig out

contrary to what some might say
you *can* dig your way out of a hole

    it takes a sculptor's eye
    to cast a glance at a wall of earth
    and spy the staircase buried within

        it takes time and effort
            patience and precision
        to carve each step
        so that it will hold you
         without crumbling beneath

        and there will be the false steps
          there will be those barred by stones
          there will be roots and tangles
        but no one moves towards the sky simply
           without sacrifice

muscles will strain
sinews will falter
a moment taken for breath
will exhale inertia

but dig on
intuit that shape which will lift you upward
shape the dirt that surrounds you into it

do not surrender
however exhausted
the future you want is always the tougher journey

but dig out
however hardscrabble the work
however high the goal may seem
because you *can't* stay where you are

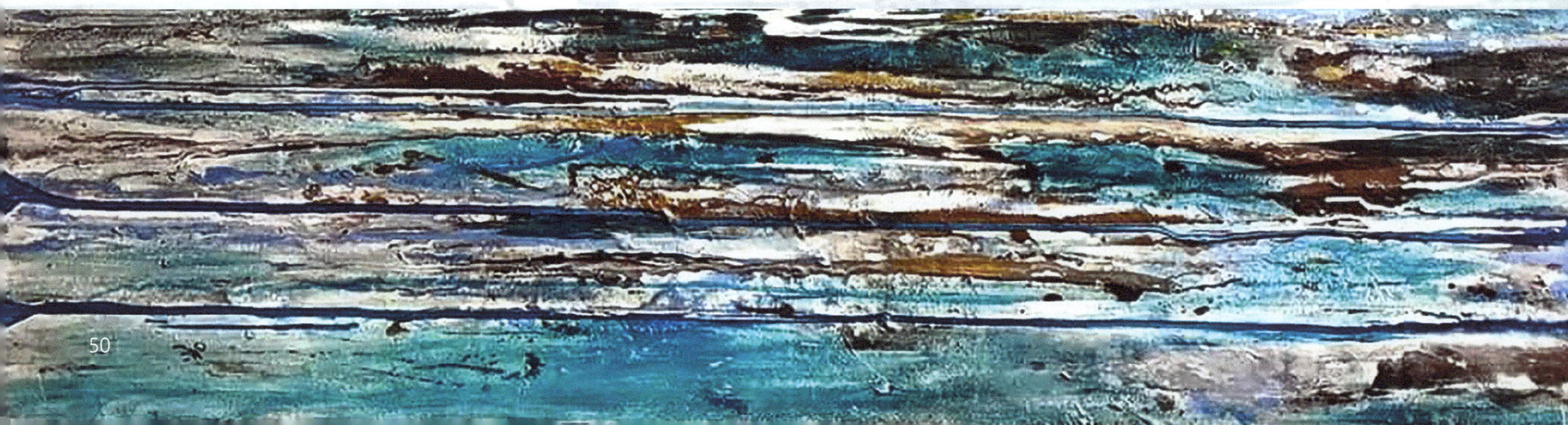

the earth might be moving
much too fast for you to keep up
  but if you choose your direction well
    it'll all come back to you

      you *can* dig your way out of a hole
        and if you do it right
      you leave a path for others to follow
        sparing them the struggle

          look around you and see the signs
          how much has been overcome
          in ways that still lift you higher
          in ways that still will
            — if you let them —
          show you the way out.

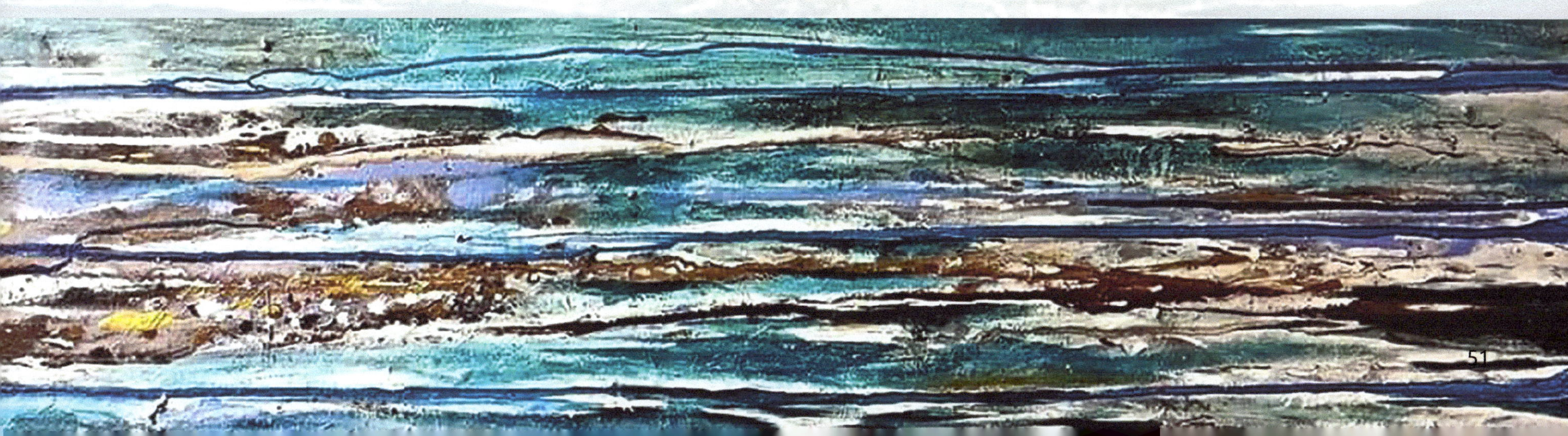

danger

there are constants
   in nature
    in time
     in human existence
and danger
    is chief among them

but it's the same as with warfare
the scope changes
   with advances in delivery systems

when knives evolve to bombs
  and whips to wages
the aggressor's prize is no longer
   a glint of fear in an eye

instead,
  it is resignation in a footfall
   a conversation in a coffeehouse
    with a tremor in the voice
  a cigarette pulled from the lips
    in anxious frustration
  a bottle drained to speed the clock
  fingers dancing on a remote control
  fat and sugar fondled by a fork

damocles had it easy
  solely one sword to suffer
  whose point drove deeper
   before breaking skin

we have missiles never seen
the final paycheque
paper bullets in window envelopes
disease driving through wind and bodily fluids
someone else's need to be there faster
mechanical marvels' myriad meltdowns
corporate need to grow
   free of remorse or regret

we talk, hear, see, and know
  more of danger
   than hope
    or joy
    or love

but if this is how we choose to live
maybe
  we have nothing left to fear.

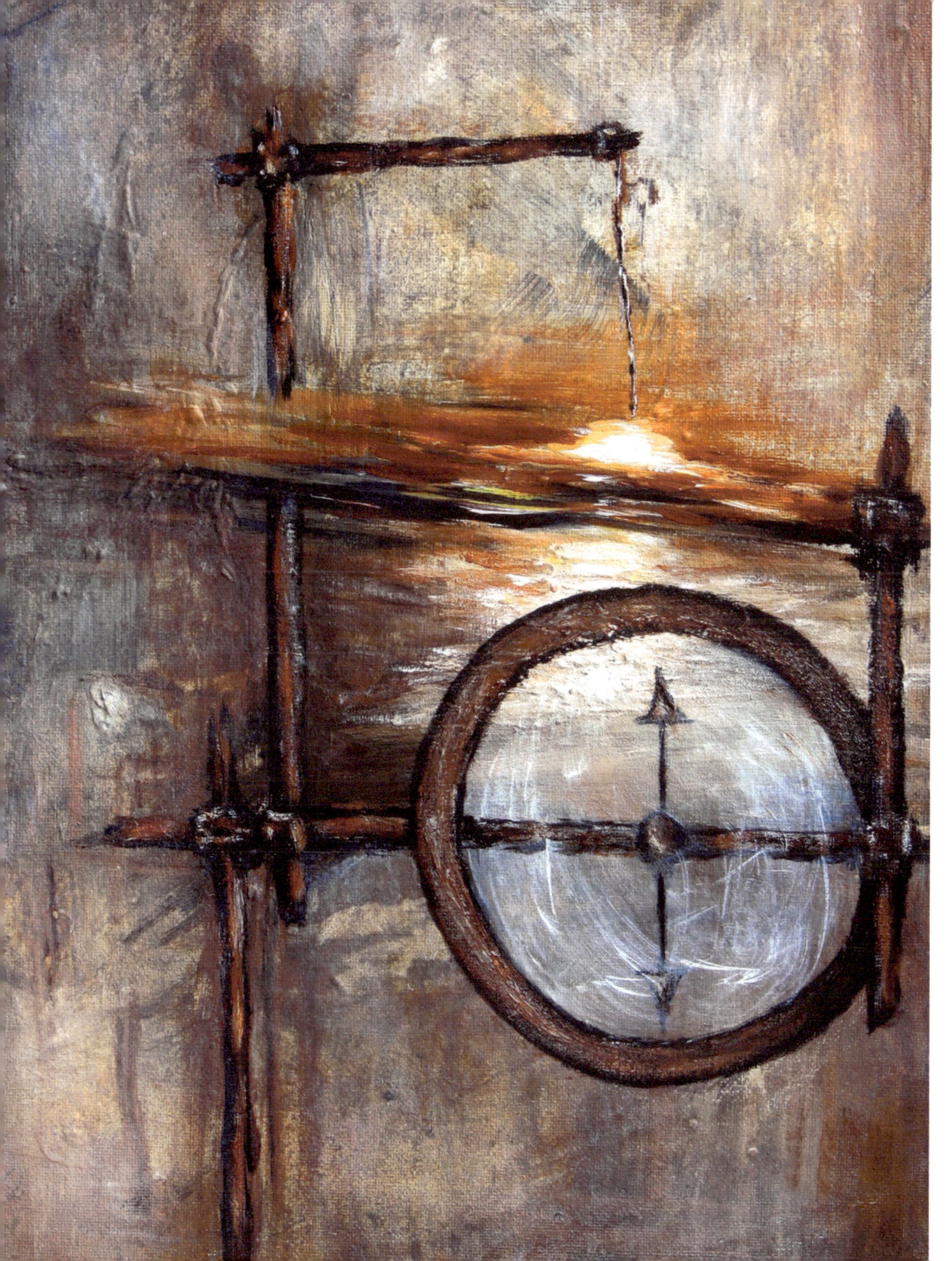

humanity 101:
final exam

Misdirection in Time

question one:
close your eyes.
assume we're on the phone.
assume i'm white.
what difference does it make?
does anything betray me?
are the paradigms i fit more comfortable
    in this frame of reference? how so?
include at least four examples from your past.

Becoming

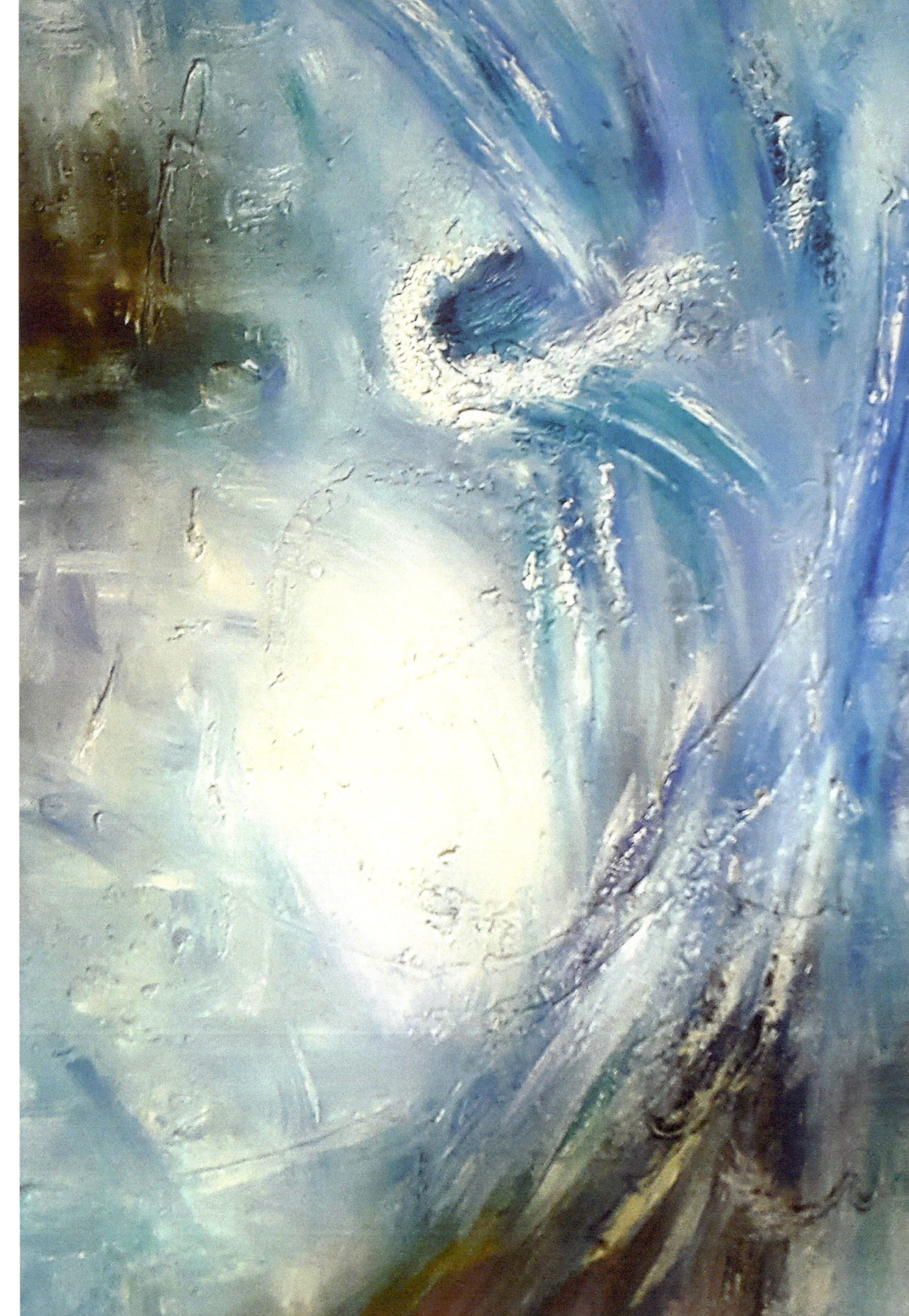

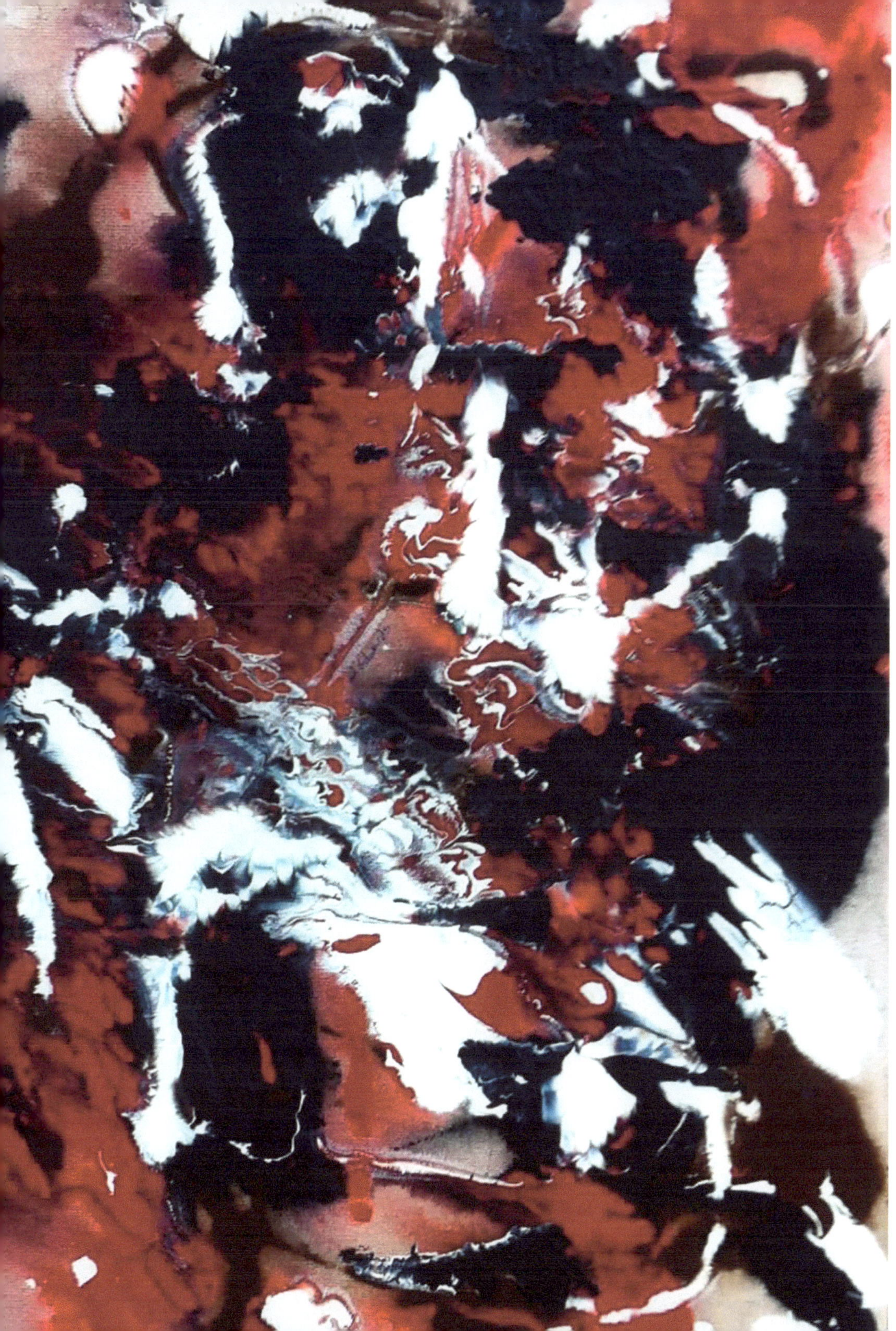

question two:
cover your ears.
assume we have just met in the street.
assume you have correctly guessed my religion.
what do you hold back?
do you ask anything you wouldn't otherwise?
are you hoping to learn something
    or just shielding your own opinions? why?
include at least three preconceptions you admit.

question three:
smile slyly.
assume we're at a bar.
assume i'm straight.
what are your motives?
do you buy me a drink?
is your body language just different
    or absent? in what way?
include at least two mistakes you have made.

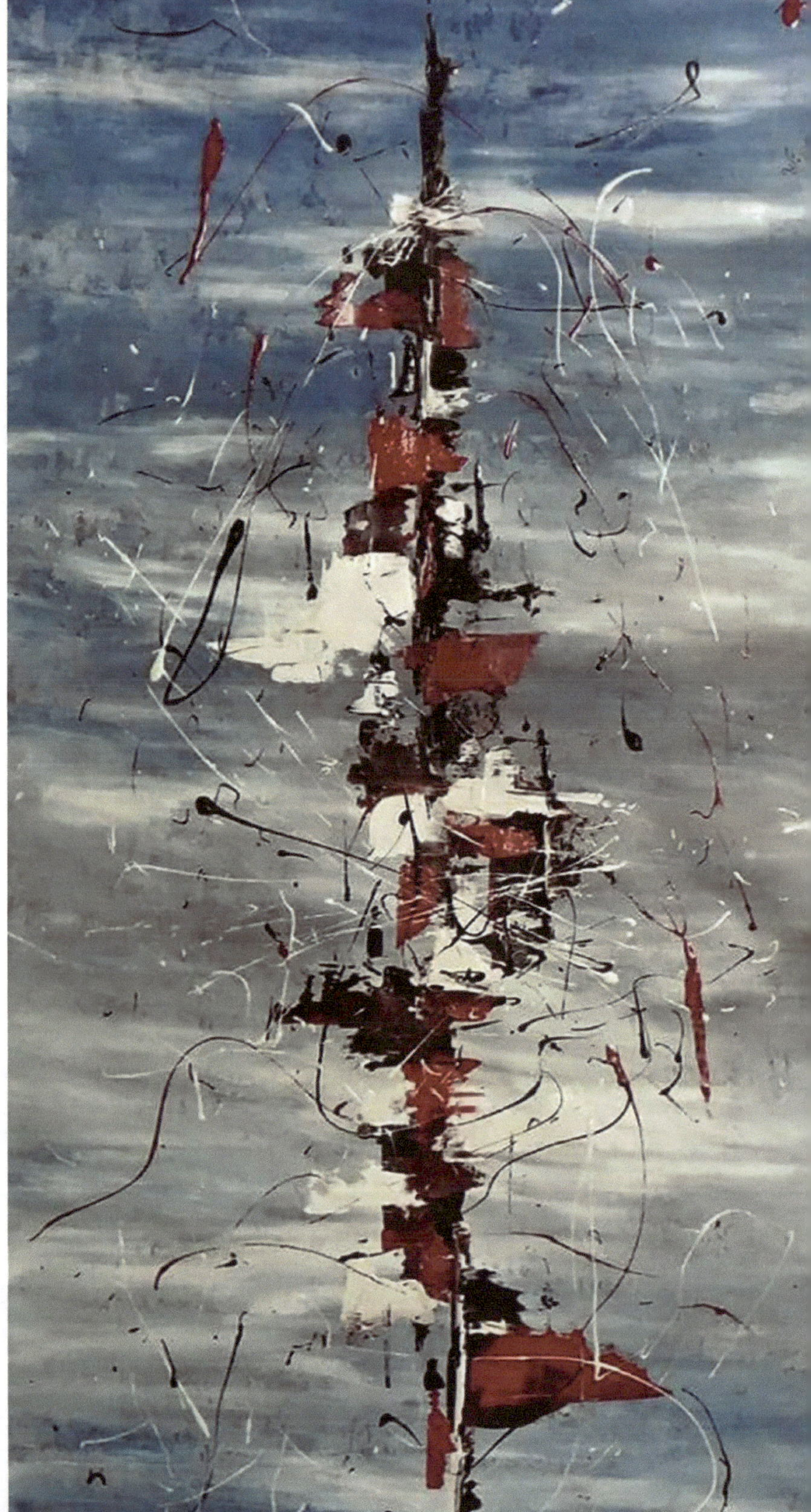

Towering

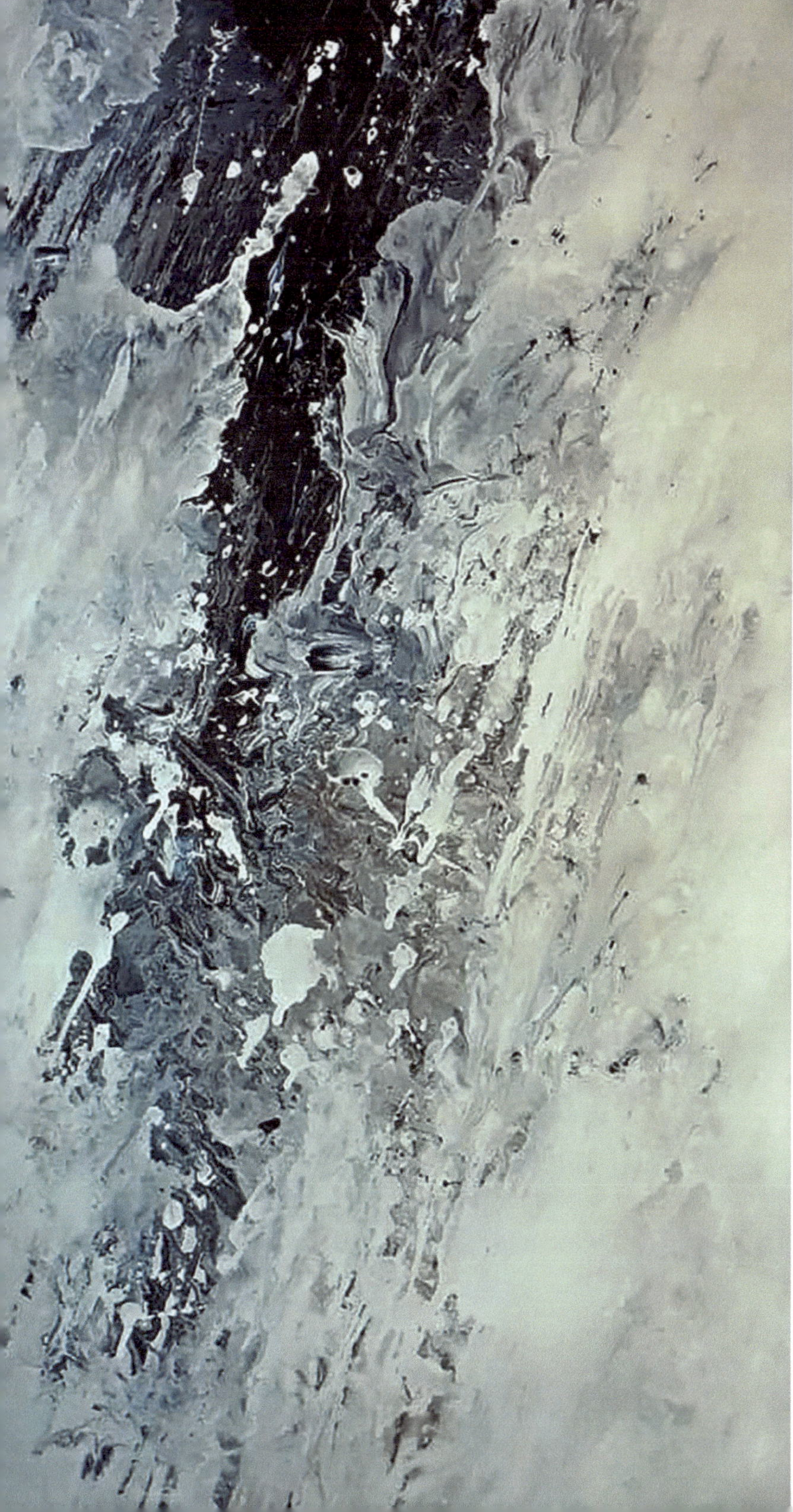

question four:
assume we're strangers,
assuming nothing.
what do we discuss?
is eye contact comfortable?
are the things left unsaid
    your loss or mine?
include at least one reason i should care.

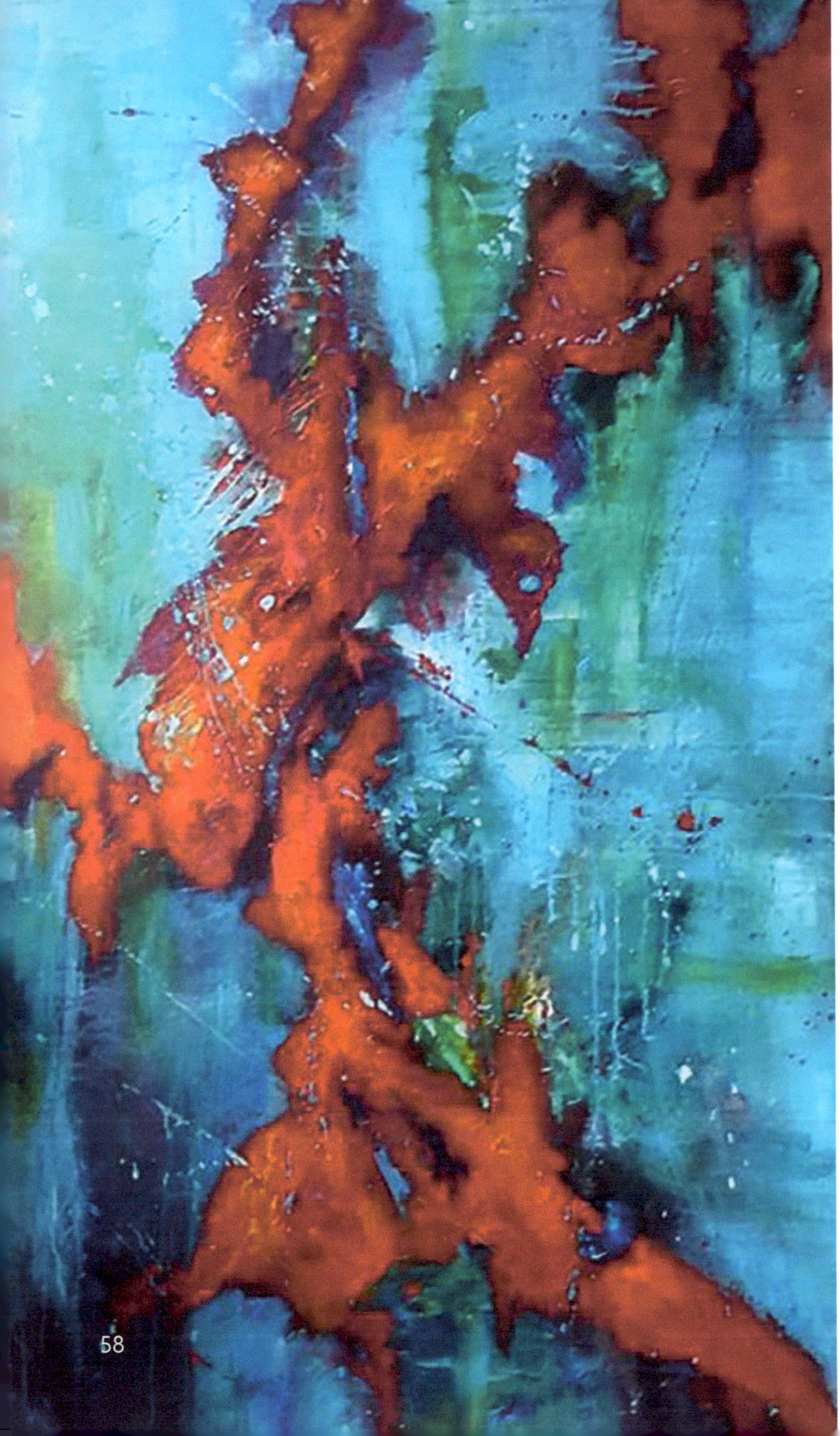

question *five:*
open your eyes.
uncover your ears.
wipe that smirk off your face.
who else is around?
can they see you?
what are the assumptions they're making
    about you right now?
include your odds of escaping predefinition.

Underwater Breathing

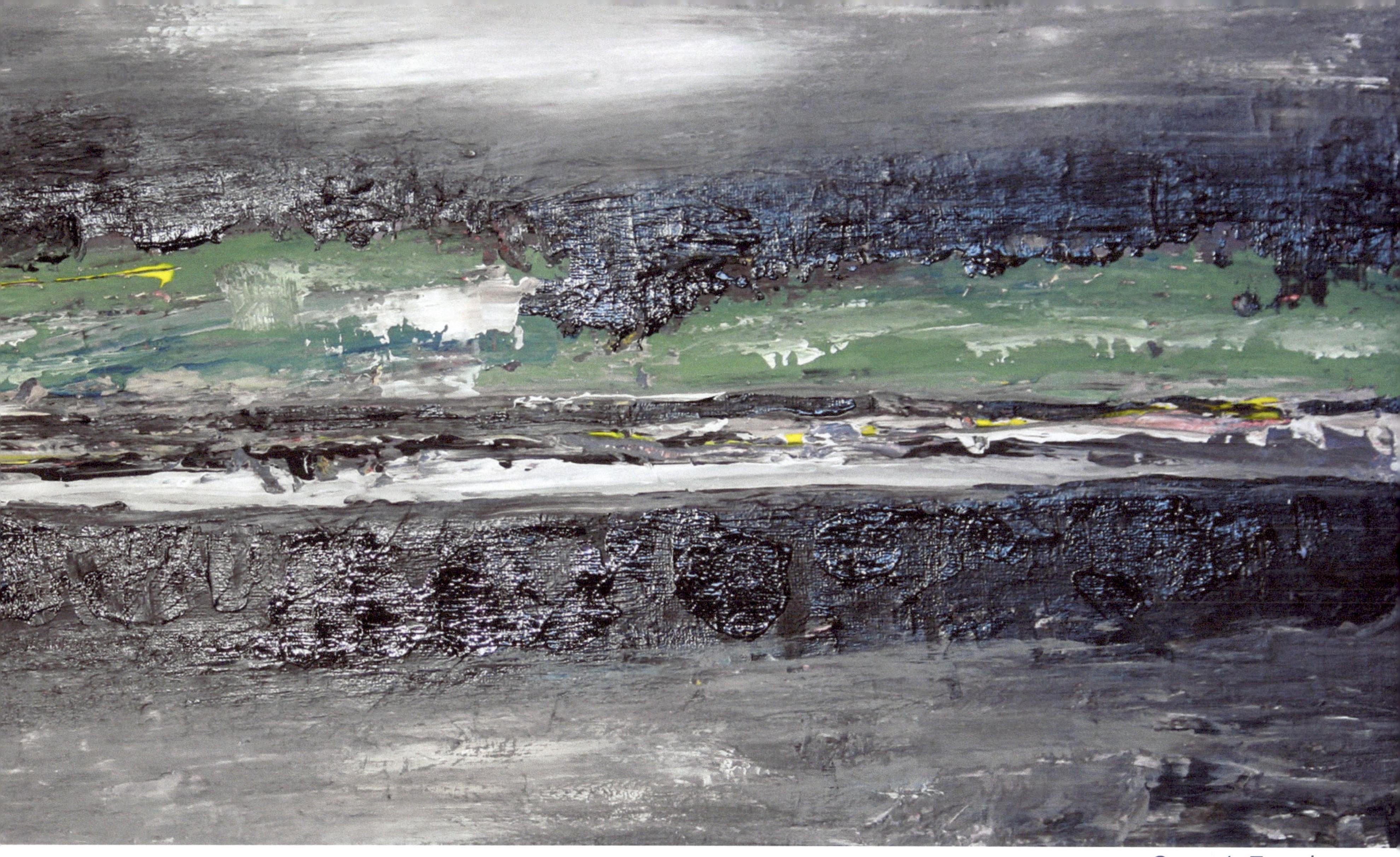

Ocean's Trend

you will be graded on your economy of language.
you will be graded on your presentation.
you will be graded on your reasoning and associations.
you will be graded on your performance
               relative to those around you.

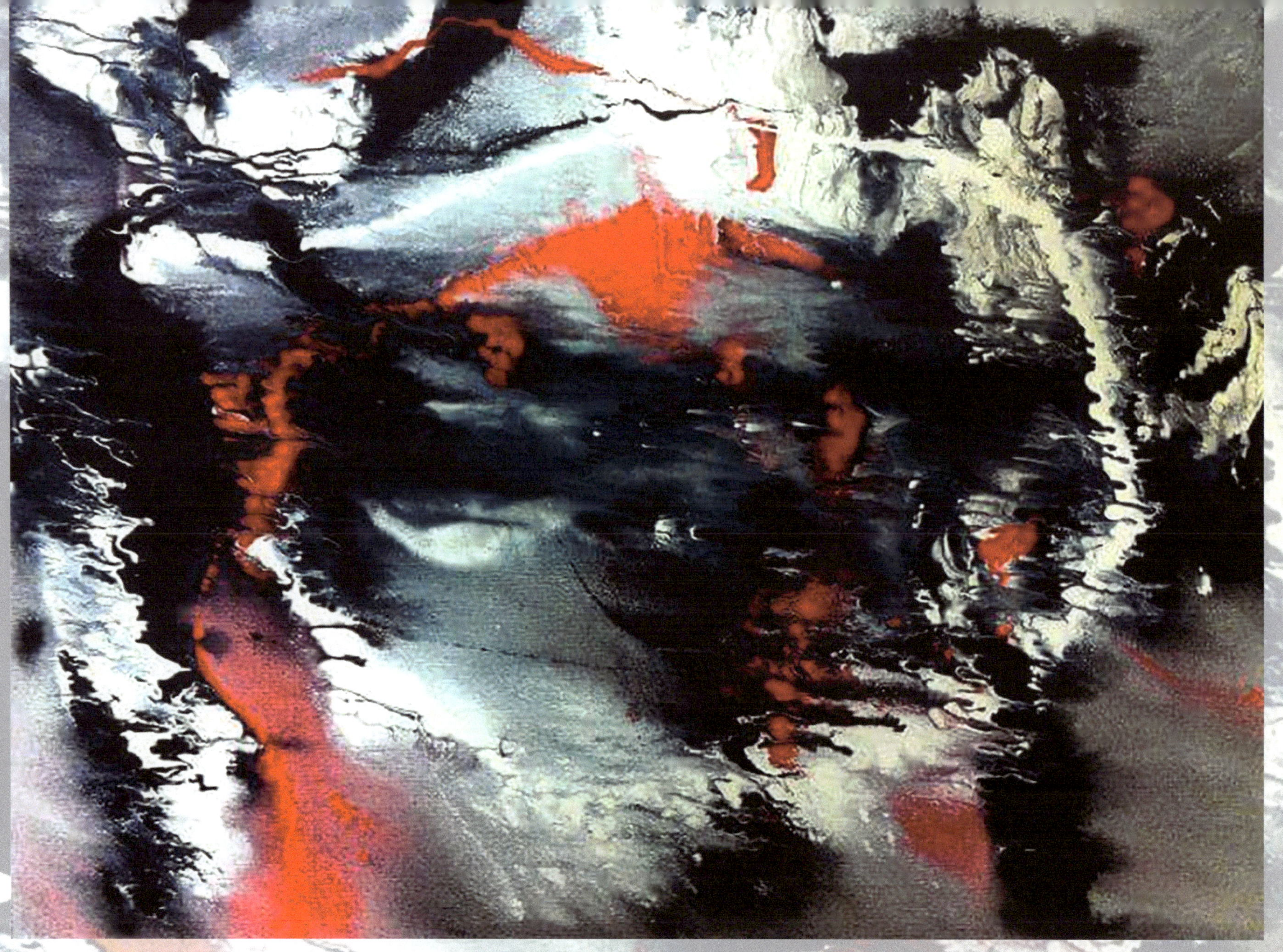

you have until death to finish this test.
you have been provided with all supplies necessary.

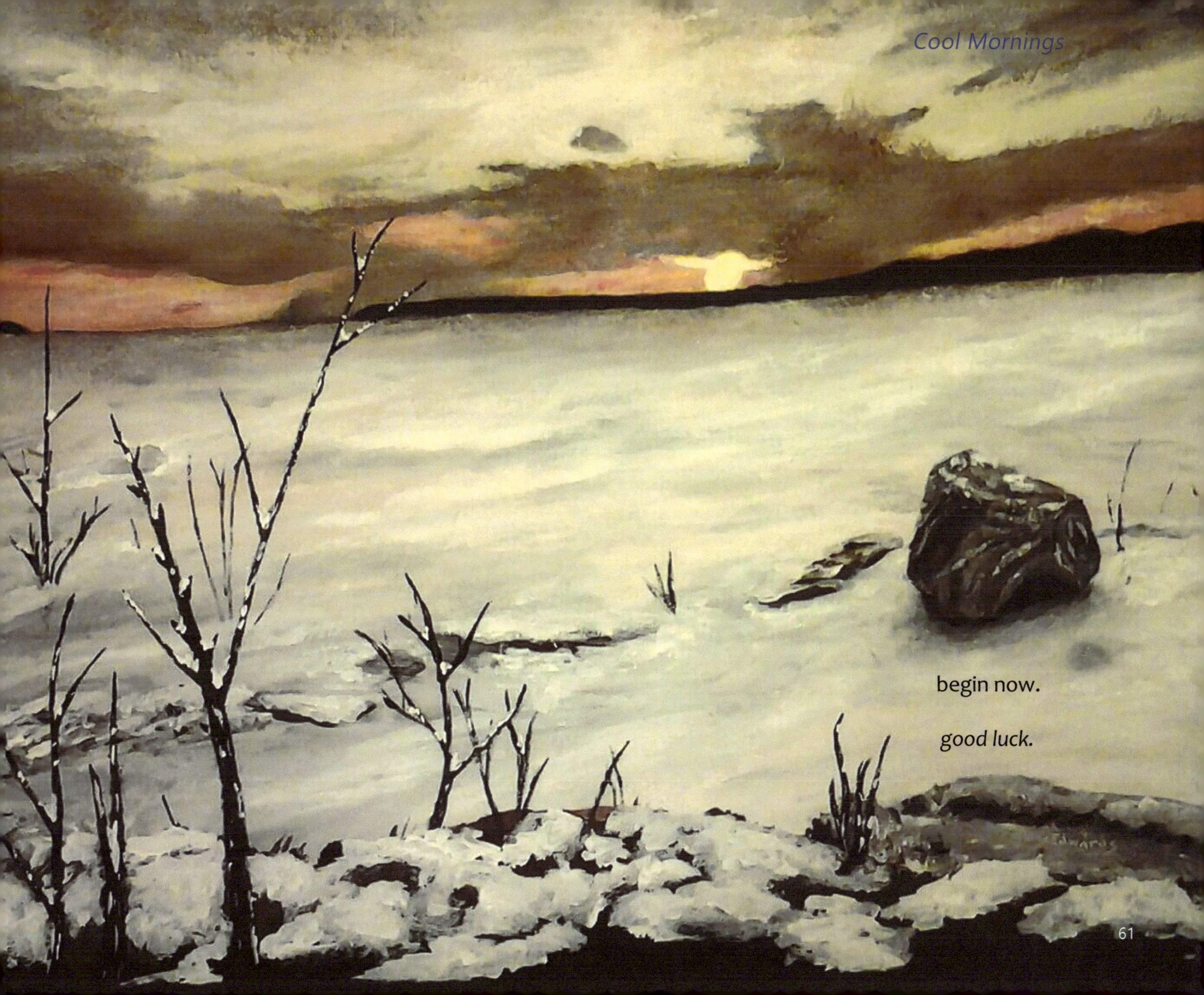
Cool Mornings
begin now.
good luck.
61

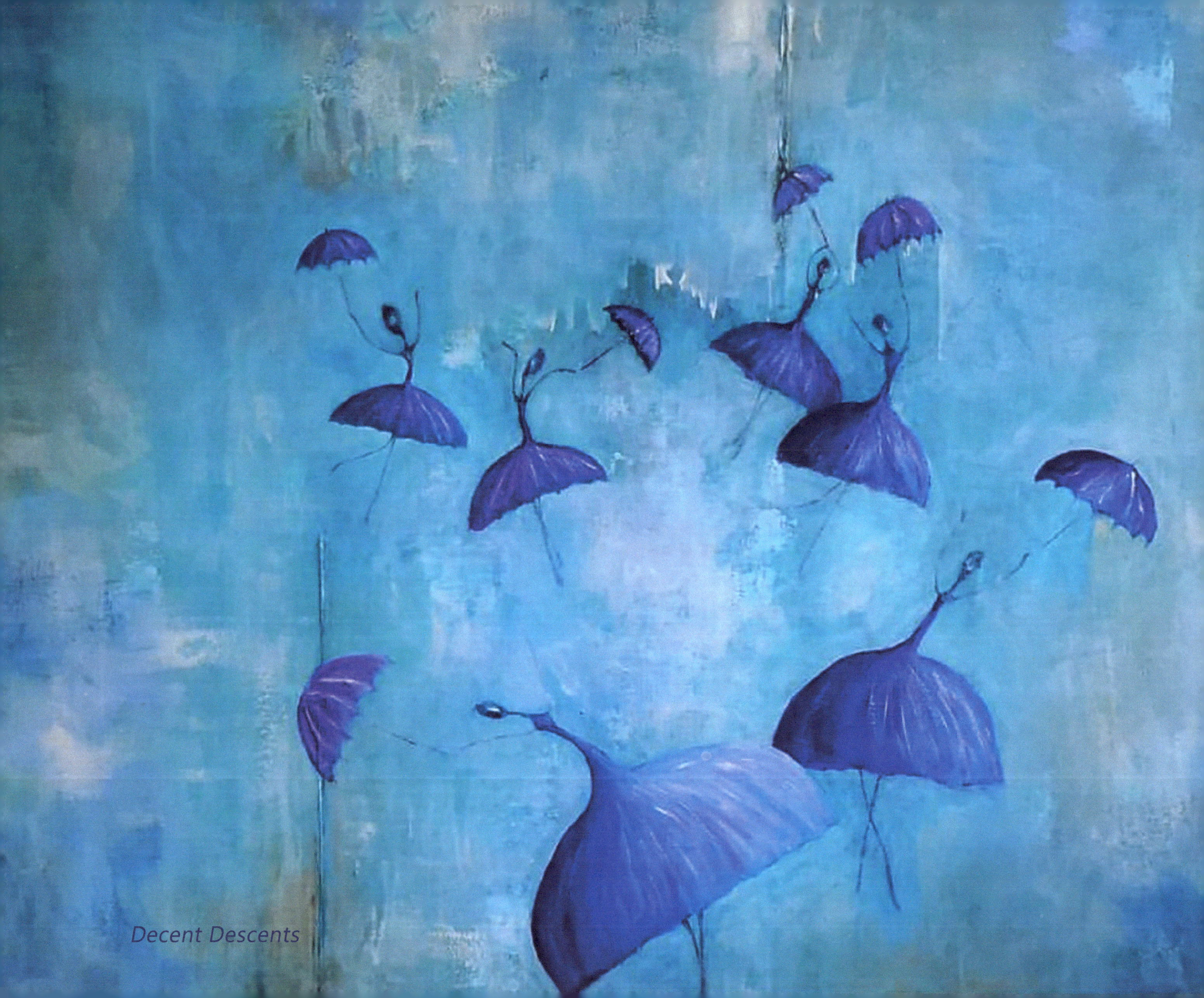
Decent Descents

About the Authors

When KYLE HAWKE was 5 and visiting India for the first time, his grandfather's circle of activist and theologian friends told him he should be a writer. That became the one expectation on him he held fast to.

Kyle has been performing spoken word since the 1990s. Preferring to perform with musicians and painters, he founded the Voice on Canvas and Bohemian Caress reading series, both of which saw performance poetry, improvised music, and live painting concurrently on stage. He's also been active with various literary non-profit groups.

Themes of identity, universality, and the moment figure significantly in Kyle's work. Working in juxtaposition with other artforms has always fascinated him, leading to many ekphrastic poems and many performances with painters and musicians. He feels that having multiple voices speak to a theme or comment on each other adds focus on what is universal, adding new context to each voice.

whispers of humanity is Kyle's first collection of poetry in book form. He lives in Vancouver, BC.

A prolific creator, WADE EDWARDS aims to examine every vantage offered by human variation. Self-taught but inspired by artists as diverse as da Vinci, Monet, and Wilson Bickford, his work explores abstract and impressionist themes through constantly shifting and evolving techniques as suits the moment and subject.

Wade has shown his work from coast to coast. He was a partner in the Avenue Gallery, the feature in-store painter for the Davie Art Shop, a regular live painter for the Bohemian Caress series, and winner of a national competition which saw his work displayed on advertising boards nationally.

Having come to the canvas later in life than many, Wade develops his own techniques as he goes. While respecting formal structures and approaches, he feels most comfortable letting his brushes be his eyes and throwing himself whole into the work. He looks forward to exploring new forms and techniques as opportunity is sparked by chance or spurred by the muses.

whispers of humanity is Wade's first published collection of paintings. He lives in Vancouver, BC.

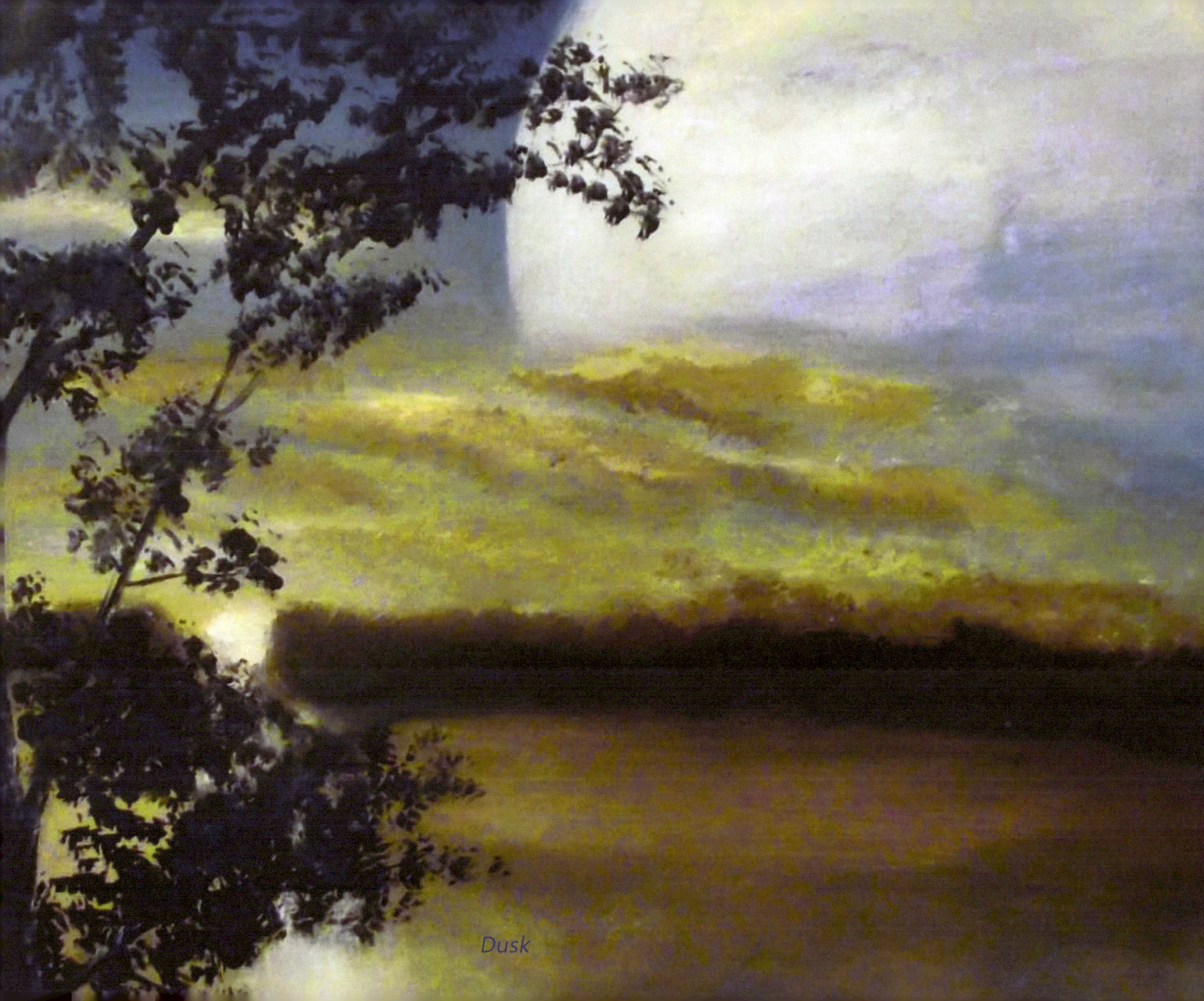
Dusk